Prince Edward Island:
An ᵁᴺAuthorized History

Prince Edward Island: An ^UN Authorized History

written by
Boyde Beck

illustrated by
P. John Burden

Acorn Press
Charlottetown, Prince Edward Island
1996

Prince Edward Island: An (Un)Authorized History

Text © 1996 by Boyde Beck
Illustrations © 1996 by P. John Burden

Book designed by Henry Dunsmore
Printed and bound in Canada by Williams & Crue, Ltd., Summerside.

10 9 8 7 6 5 4 3 2

Canadian Cataloguing in Publication Data

Beck, Boyde.
  Prince Edward Island
  ISBN 0-9698606-1-7

1. Prince Edward Island — History. I. Burden, P. John, 1943-
II. Title.
FC2611.B42 1996   971.7   C96-950070-X   F1048.B42 1996

Published by
The Acorn Press
P.O. Box 22024
Charlottetown, Prince Edward Island
C1A 9J2

I would most respectfully beg your leave to
dedicate this book to my wife, Anna.
— Boyde Beck

To my Master, Henry Wilkinson.
— P. John Burden

Contents

Preface

You know, in a way the histories of Prince Edward Island are a lot like quantum physics. Over the past decades there have been great advances in research. The frontiers of knowledge are pushed ever forward. Theories old and new abound. Yet, practitioners still wait for someone to come up with a grand, unifying theory — a single, all-encompassing work that will take many disparate strands and weave them into a simple, coherent, comprehensive whole.

This ain't it.

My best friend and sometimes-mentor likes to say that the most important part of the word "history" is "story." Stories about the people, the places, the things and events that give shape and definition to the past of a place. Sometimes the stories aren't too neat and tidy. And sometimes the endings aren't particularly happy. But that's what this book is. Stories. About some of the people, places, things and events that define the past of this place. And they do share a common thread. They're all interesting.

At least, *I* think they are.

Mount Stewart
Prince Edward Island
1996

Acknowledgements

This book had its genesis in a regular history spot that CBC Charlottetown's *MainStreet* program invited me to do. To paraphrase Dr. Johnson, nothing focuses the mind so wonderfully as knowing you have only twelve minutes to tell your story. So, many thanks to Sheryl MacKay, Nils Ling, Karen Mair, Leslie Goldstone and Whit Carter, who helped me learn the techniques of good story-telling, and allowed me to practice live and on air.

Thanks also to the staff at Robertson Library and the Public Archives and Records Office, for letting me wander through their collections.

Thank you, Ed, both for letting me bounce ideas off your head and for keeping me on the historical straight and narrow.

And, finally, I would like to thank the cats, for keeping me company while I wrote, and for keeping their keesters off the keyboard.

And no. I didn't make any of this stuff up. I labouriously researched each and every chapter, meticulously checking and double-checking each and every single fact. A task greatly aided, I must confess, by the scads of excellent research and writing contained in *The Island Magazine* and the *Dictionary of Canadian Biography*. As a matter of fact, were it not for the aforementioned *Magazine* and *Dictionary*, I would still be labouriously researching many of the chapters in this book. Other volumes that have been heavily leaned upon include J. M. Bumsted's *Land, Settlement and Politics*, D. C. Harvey's *The French Regime on Prince Edward Island* and *Journeys to the Island of Saint John*, and Basil Greenhill's *Westcountrymen in Prince Edward's Isle*. Original research (i.e., the stuff I wasn't able to plunder from other people's work) was conducted through the newspapers and archival sources available at the Public Archives and Records Office, and UPEI's Robertson Library.

So, as some say down home: If it's a lie from me, it was a lie to me!

By Any Other Name...

 chronic headache for Island historians is keeping the name of the place straight. The Mi'kmaq, as any reader of the official tourist guide can tell you, called the place "Abegweit."[1] It would have been so much simpler if the early Europeans settling here had stuck with that. Instead they had to customize it. Jacques Cartier, the first European to officially "discover" the Island, named it after St. Jean, the saint whose day he discovered it on.

When the British took the place from the French, they simply Anglicized the name. "Île St. Jean" became St. John's Island. But by the 1770s, it was apparent that there were too many "Saint Johns" in the Gulf of St.

---

[1] Or "Minagoo," which was apparently more common but less melodic. Which is why the official tourist guide prefers Abegweit.

Lawrence. A river, a valley, two major settlements and an entire colony. It was just too confusing. Walter Patterson, the Island's first Governor, made the first attempt at clarification. He passed a law changing the name to "New Ireland." This was very fitting, since he and the majority of his officials were Anglo-Irish. But London didn't take to the idea. It was not the place of a minor colonial governor, it informed Patterson, to go around changing the official names of places. Besides, Ireland was not the sort of place British officialdom wanted to see honoured on a map.

London did agree, though, that a name change would be useful. It suggested "New Guernsey," or perhaps "New Anglesea." Charlottetown's response to this was not recorded. Perhaps its silence was comment enough.

The matter was let rest until the 1790s. Then a different colonial administration made another attempt. It suggested the place be named after Prince Edward, the Duke of Kent. One of George III's younger sons, Kent was one of the first members of a European Royal Family to actually live in the New World. In the 1790s he was serving as the senior naval officer in Halifax. He never visited the Island. In fact, the only time he ever mentioned the place was in a recommendation it be re-annexed to Nova Scotia. But the name change was approved, and on July 1, 1799, St. John's Island became Prince Edward Island.

So the rule of thumb goes like this. If you're talking Mi'kmaq era, it's Abegweit. Or Minagoo. Between 1534 and 1760 or so, you can use Île St. Jean. Between 1760 and 1799, St. John's Island will do. After 1799 you refer to Prince Edward Island. Or, play it safe, do what most Islanders do, and just call it "the Island." Because...

"What other Island is there?"

The Battle of the Northeast River

I t's late June, 1745. A half company of British troops cruise up what we call the Hillsborough River. They're conducting an invasion, and it's coming along very nicely. In fact, they're probably feeling quite smug. Barely a week before, they watched as the supposedly invincible fortress of Louisbourg surrendered to their army. Now they've been detached to mop up the tiny outpost on Île St. Jean. Most of the soldiers hail from New England. From childhood they've been taught a healthy hatred for their French neighbours to the north. They must be taking a particular delight with how easily things are going.

Compared to the rest of North America, the Island was a late addition to the list of places Britain and France considered worth fighting for. To the best of our knowledge, the French were the first Europeans to take an interest in the Island.[1] Their era here began in 1534 when Jacques Cartier sighted, logged, named and claimed Île St. Jean for the French King. The latter was no doubt grateful, but didn't seem to have an immediate use for the place.

In the late 1600s, small factions at the French Court made a hobby of fighting for exclusive rights to the Island. They thought Île St. Jean would make a fine fishing base. Some even had dreams of colonizing the place. But even though the Island was given to, then taken from, a series of patrons, no one actually did anything with it. Which no doubt suited the actual occupants just fine.

French colonial efforts in the Gulf of St. Lawrence centred on mainland Acadia — modern-day Nova Scotia.

---

[1] It's entirely possible that the Norse, the Basques or John Cabot visited at an earlier date, but if they did, they failed to leave a calling card.

Though the Island was usually considered part of that colony, few Acadians showed much interest in settling here. But in the early 1700s, French colonial policy was turned on its head. After a poor showing in the War of the Spanish Succession (1701-1713), it lost mainland Acadia to Great Britain. Île St. Jean, Île Royale (Cape Breton), and a few other small islands were all France had left in the Gulf of St. Lawrence.

France's plans to rebuild its Gulf colonies were simple. It would erect a mighty fortress — Louisbourg — on Île Royale. This would guard the entrance to the Gulf and access to the more important colonies up the St. Lawrence River. It would also allow France to dominate the lucrative fishing grounds in this part of the world. The former population of Acadia would relocate to Île St. Jean, which was suddenly being touted as the Granary of New France. These stalwart farmers would grow the food to feed the fortress that would make New France impervious to assault. As the world's best military engineers got to work, officials at the French Court congratulated themselves for their cleverness and foresight. They only made one oversight.

No one thought to tell the Acadians.

Back on the mainland, the Acadians had been building their settlements for over a century. They compared the inconvenience of uprooting themselves to the odium of living under British rule. Since Britain offered an unprecedented degree of freedom to live their lives and practice their religion, most Acadians decided to take their chances with the British.[2]

When the flood of Acadians failed to materialize, France decided to give the process a kick-start by assigning a commandant and sending a garrison and civil administrators to build the infrastructure no European settler was comfortable without. In 1724 the latter landed and, in a fit of good cheer, decided to call the capital Port La Joye. Slowly, the settlers began to arrive and a handful of small villages took root.

Through the 1730s, though, the French on the Island must have thought they'd been cursed. Forest fire, crop failure and mouse infestations of Biblical proportions on several occasions forced the Granary of

---

[2] Don't make the mistake of confusing the downright vicious decision of 1755 to expel the Acadians with the politics of earlier British administrations. At first, Britain was remarkably kind and gentle — as foreign conquerors go. In 1720, for instance, French-speaking, Roman Catholic Acadians enjoyed more rights and freedoms than did Gaelic-speaking Scots or Protestant Dissenters like Quakers and Baptists. It wasn't until the 1730s that things began to turn nasty for Britain's Acadians.

New France to request emergency supplies from Louisbourg. But by the 1740s things were beginning to look up. More Acadians were emigrating from British Nova Scotia, and the European population was pushing fifteen hundred settlers. The fishery was prosperous and the colony's farmers had recorded three successful harvests in a row.

Then, back in Europe, Louis XV of France decided a cousin of his

Then he waxed their fannies.

should be the new King of Austria. Great Britain objected. France responded. As militaries across the continent wheezed into life, it was decided to call it The War of the Austrian Succession.[3]

The British colonies in New England were delighted for any opportunity to smash up some of their New French neighbours. This might seem like mean-spirited paranoia, but look at the situation like this. New England considered itself a small enclave surrounded by the hostile and unknown. To the west were impenetrable mountains and unknown native tribes. (Remember, west meant anything over four hundred kilometres from the Atlantic coast.) To the south were the older, and, at least on paper, more powerful colonies of New Spain — a traditional enemy. To the north was New France, the oldest enemy of all. Add to this the bland assurance that God was a New Englishman, and their unneighbourly attitude is easier to explain. Unfortunately, New England's love of a good imperial dust-up always resulted in bad things for New France.

It's not that French armies were incompetent. It's just that Great Britain always took the North American segment of its wars more seriously than France did. As the unfinished and undermanned Louisbourg tottered toward surrender, the French colonists on Île St. Jean knew they could count on little help from the Mother Country.

The British company sent to seize the colony had a choice of three targets. The colony's metropolis was St. Pierre. A fishing port on the north shore but with fairly easy river access to the capital, St. Pierre housed nearly half of the European population. Down the eastern coast was Trois Rivières, a private colony set up by Jean-Pierre Roma. The Colony's nerve centre, of course, was Port La Joye. Expecting little resistance, the British divided their force, sending half to Trois Rivières, half to Port La Joye.

The first two battles went fairly smoothly. At Trois Rivières, Sieur DeRoma considered his artillery (one, old, worn six-pounder), surveyed his garrison (which consisted mainly of his son and daughter), and decided he'd had enough of Île St. Jean. Taking to the woods, he made his way to St. Pierre and boarded the first vessel to Quebec. He never came back.

The British also found Port La Joye completely undefended. The garrison, according to the best intelligence, had beat it upriver as soon as they'd seen the British coming. Pausing to burn the capital to the

---

[3] It was at this point the editors insisted I resist the urge to observe that wars in this era seemed to arrive "in succession."

ground — not the hardest of jobs, given that most of the buildings were falling down anyway — they set off in pursuit of the retreating French. The campaign was now quite simple. Catch the French garrison, thrash it, then carry on to St. Pierre and burn it. At that point Île St. Jean could be declared well and truly conquered.

The French forces were under the command of François Dupont Duvivier. He'd been left in charge when the Commandant was summoned to take over the defences at Louisbourg.[4] He viewed his progress upriver as a strategic retreat, and was determined to get his troops away to Quebec, where they might do some good. Along the way he supplemented his forces with a handful of settlers and a number of Mi' kmaq, whom French governors had always been careful to treat well. Somewhere along the river he turned to face the advancing British.

Then he waxed their fannies. The strategy and tactics were never recorded. No one even thought to remember exactly where on the river it took place. But it was the bloodiest battle in Island history. Before the stunned New Englanders could scramble back to their boats, twenty-eight had been killed, wounded or captured. It might seem like small potatoes, but there have been battles not much bigger that at least rate a name.

The battle of the Northeast River probably isn't remembered because it didn't change anything. The British might have lost the engagement, but they'd already won control of the Gulf. Île St. Jean was theirs by default. Duvivier knew this, and used his victory merely to buy the time he needed to get away to Quebec. In the truce that followed, the French on the Island promised not to attack any more British expeditions,[5] and the British generously promised not to burn down any more French settlements.

In 1749, Great Britain traded Île St. Jean and Île Royale back to France in return for a small city in India. Life for the Island's Acadians returned to normal.

Until the next time somebody threw a war.

---

[4] This lucky soul arrived just in time to take responsibility for surrendering the fortress.

[5] The next year, somebody on the French side goofed and ambushed a large party of New Englanders who had landed to buy provisions. The total this time was over forty killed, wounded or captured. The victorious French were profuse in their apologies, and nothing further came of the incident.

Lotto 1767

It seemed like such a good idea at the time. In 1763, after a very good showing in the Seven Years' War, Great Britain found itself with half a continent full of new colonies. Since experience had shown the rule to be "use them, or lose them," it was vital to get the new territories settled as expediently as possible. There was only one problem — the treasury was almost empty. Britain was discovering that the only thing more expensive than building an empire was maintaining it.

A new colony required huge start-up costs. First you had to attract settlers, then transport them, then keep them from starving while they carved their farms out of the forest. Then you had to build roads and harbours and churches and jails. You had to hire a governor. And people to collect taxes. And people to arrest the people who didn't pay their taxes. And people to put the tax revenues in the bank. And people to make sure that all the people maintaining the tax system got paid. And so on. Civilization just didn't grow on trees, you know. It took a lot of hard work — and money — to get things started off right.

Then someone came up with a wonderful idea.

Why not let the private sector do it? The new territories could be made to pay their own way, if the right investors could be found. All that was needed was a place to try the idea out. A colonial case study, if you will.

St. John's Island was an ideal candidate. The French had described it as "The Granary of New France." The new masters quickly converted this to "The Granary of British North America." At a time when kingdoms were judged more by the strength of their farms than their industries, this was high praise indeed. The Island could easily support a population of five hundred thousand. It had the best farmland on the continent — or so the buzz

St. John's Island
and
Surveyor-General
Samual Holland

P. John Burden

By the summer of 1767 everything was in place.

went. Even better, thanks to the efforts of the British armed forces, the previous European occupants had already been turfed out.[1] Of all the King's new North American possessions, this one was the ripest for exploitation.

John Percival, the second Earl of Egmont, devised the first scheme. He asked that the King grant him the entire Island, which he proposed to run as his personal fief. In return for complete authority, he promised to give the King a prosperous colony and a fixed number of well-trained soldiers whenever requested. Some of Egmont's contemporaries — and many later historians — dismissed him as a lunatic with delusions of feudal grandeur. But the proposal was given serious treatment at the time.

At the heart of Egmont's scheme was the promise to relieve the Crown from the risks involved in developing a colony, while passing on a portion of the revenue it generated. Soon a more workable scheme was circulating. The Island could be divided into twenty-thousand-acre parcels. The parcels would be granted to anyone interested in and capable of developing them. Successful grantees would promise to clear and settle their land to a certain ratio within ten years, and remit "quit"[2] rents annually to the Crown. The revenue generated by these quit rents would go toward building and supporting a civil infrastructure. The grantees, in turn, would make their income from renting farmland to the flood of emigrants just itching to try their hand in the New World. Thus, in jig time the Island would be up and functioning as a productive member of the Empire. And at no cost to the over-strained Treasury.

The plan was submitted to the Lords Commissioners for Trade and Plantations — precursor to what would become the Colonial Office. They suggested a few alterations. As a gesture to Lord Egmont, he was offered an extra-large parcel of one hundred thousand acres. This he refused — if he couldn't have it all, he wanted nothing more to do with the place. The Lords Commissioners also insisted that prospective proprietors guarantee they would settle their lands with "foreign Protestants." Population was considered a strategic reserve, and Britain considered itself under-populated — especially when compared to mighty France. It didn't want its colonies to drain vital manpower away. British authorities had also concluded, through their experience in trying to rule Acadians and Highland Scots, that Catholics could become espe-

---

[1] In 1758, British policy toward its Acadian subjects took a cruel turn when it was decided to deport the entire population from the Gulf of St. Lawrence region.

[2] Quit rents were just what they said — pay the rent or quit the property.

cially bothersome subjects. With these minor modifications in place, the Island of St. John's no-pain settlement scheme was set into motion. Surveys were assembled, and the Government began to gather a list of worthy candidates it felt beholden to.

By the summer of 1767 everything was in place. Surveyor-General Samuel Holland submitted a plan subdividing the Island into counties, parishes and sixty-seven lots — each more or less the required twenty-thousand acres. Since there were more interested candidates than lots, it was decided to hold a lottery. On July 23 the names were put into a hat and the Island received sixty-seven — more or less — new owners. The British Era had begun.

The Land Question was born.

Walter Patterson

Imagine yourself in a room 40 feet long and 25 feet high. The cabinet ministers are sitting on red velvet covered chairs along a green covered table. The rest of the room is full of spectators, for curiosity excites many to be present. On that day the council chamber is an aweful sight. I never saw Mr. Patterson look so ill.

— John MacDonald to his
sister Helen, 1790

Every Island historian has to overcome the temptation to consider Mr. Patterson the father of our country. It's so enticing.

He was our first post-conquest governor. He demanded and received the right to treat the Island as a colony separate from Nova Scotia. (Just ask a Cape Bretoner how important *that* is.) He was the first to punish those who had not fulfilled the terms of their original grant agreements. The first to raise the cry "Escheat!" He was also a thief of astonishing audacity. Which, history-wise, isn't a *bad* thing. But he got caught.

Which, history-wise, is not a forgivable sin.

Walter Patterson first came to North America as a soldier during the Seven Years' War. An Irish-born soldier, he got in good with the ruling party in London. As a reward for his services here and there, he was awarded half of Lot 19 in the 1767 land lottery. In 1769 he was named the colony's Governor and won its creation as a separate, independent colony. In 1770 he arrived in his new dominion.

You must remember. In 1770 the colony was elegant in theory, but lacking in execution. The European population numbered around three hundred, mostly Acadians missed by the deportation of 1758. (No one bothered to count the Mi'kmaq, but they were estimated to number two to three hundred.) Charlottetown, the colonial capital, was a hamlet consisting of a few log huts and earthworks.

By 1775 the European population had grown to a thousand, but there was still no sign that most of the original land-grantees were serious about meeting the conditions of their grants. Government officials were living on a fraction of their promised salaries. Some, like John Duport, were actually dying at their desks. Re-annexation to Nova Scotia was looming. Governor Patterson decided to go to London to sort things out.

He came back with two concessions. London agreed to pay a portion of the salary roll for the Island's administrators. It also gave Patterson permission to "take proper measures" to get back rents out of recalcitrant proprietors. Patterson returned to the colony in 1780 and quickly began the process to confiscate properties that were in arrears of their quit rents.

It's November 15, 1781.

At least we think so — the exact date was secret. Governor Patterson and a select group have gathered at John Clark's Tavern to participate in the first ever sale of defaulted lots. The only bidders present are government officials. No money changes hands — winning bidders get their land in lieu of back wages. At the end of the day, Patterson himself walks away with one hundred and seventy thousand acres. Almost half of the colony has changed hands. You have to wonder, how many who walked away from Clark's Tavern that evening knew what storm was about to break?

It's pretty well agreed that Walter Patterson made no fewer than four major mistakes that day.

First, he glommed too much for himself. This aroused suspicion.

Second, he was too greedy for improved land. If he had attacked only those many proprietors who had done nothing in the past decade to improve their holdings, he may have gotten away with it. But he also seized the land of the few resident proprietors who were genuinely trying to bring out settlers. These men had sunk a lot of money into their investments. They were very teed off when the CEO of the Colony tried to steal their investments.

Third, he didn't throw enough morsels to his cronies. There were many in the colony who hated Patterson, but who would have gone along with his coup, if there had been more in it for them. As it was,

An inquiry found him entirely at fault.

they felt cheated. If the Patterson Administration had been able to present a more or less united front of resident landowners, it might have been able to get away with it.

Finally, Patterson messed with John MacDonald. MacDonald was probably the most active landowner in the colony in 1780, and when the first writs came out, he was under the impression that his entire holding was in forfeit. This was not true, even though the Governor had been sorely tempted to swipe the rich Tracadie estate. But even after he found his land was safe, the Glenaladale remained annoyed, and he devoted the next five years to bringing Patterson down.

By the mid-1780s, Walter Patterson found himself isolated. As MacDonald rallied resistance in London, he found his support on the Island evaporating. In 1786 he was replaced by Edmund Fanning. In an epic of forgetfulness, Patterson mislaid the despatch replacing him for the better part of a year. Even after he was officially dismissed as Governor, Patterson held on. As the owner of a hundred and seventy thousand acres he was, after all, one of the chief proprietors on the Island.

By 1789 the jig was up. Walter Patterson was requested to return his tush to London to answer questions about what exactly had gone on in 1781. He hoped he'd be able to salvage his prestige and property. Not surprisingly, an inquiry found him entirely at fault, and nominated him scapegoat for the whole affair. He was severely reprimanded, but avoided a prison term. But the fortune so painstakingly built was lost, as was the career as a colonial administrator. In 1798 Walter Patterson died, a bankrupt and broken man.

> *He rose from nothing, and would have done extremely well, had he known where to stop, but the being too successful has led him constantly to go too far. Indeed, he could not have gone so far, but in such a place as St. John's Island.*
> — John MacDonald to his sister Helen, 1790

Thomas Curtis'
Excellent Adventure

In 1775 young Thomas Curtis was working in London when he met a man named Robert Clark. Clark was trying to recruit settlers for a settlement he was developing in North America. The settlement — optimistically named New London — was on the north shore of St. John's Island.

Clark spun a marvellous vision of the prospects the colony offered. On discovering Curtis had experience as a sawyer, he described boundless timberland — cheap to rent and even cheaper to buy. The growing colony was starved for lumber, giving all the market a sawyer could desire. If he didn't feel like going into business for himself, employment was plentiful and at better wages than in England. If he was inclined to farming, he would find land so fertile the crops grew themselves. Wildlife abounded. Why, you could bag a bird for breakfast through your bedroom window. Land another for lunch while you worked without even breaking rhythm.

"Such a favourable acc[t] from so respected a gentleman," Curtis recalled, "I suck[d] like sack,[1] Nay Don't think if anyone would have given me £500 I would have been satisfied to stay in London." The next day he began to arrange a passage.

He was apparently a little better off than the average emigrant — able to quickly raise £20 to pay for his passage and supplies. In addition to food for the voyage,[2] he stocked up with four dozen white shirts, six assorted firearms, a few hundred pounds of powder, the same

---

[1] Sack in this instance being a sort of sweet wine — not edible burlap.
[2] Two barrels of beef, two barrels of flour and a hundred bottles of porter, cider and rum.

amount of shot and a selection of saws. What he wasn't able to use, he reasoned, he should be able to sell. He then engaged a servant, Harry Roberts, to accompany him on the trip. Two weeks after his conversation with Robert Clark, Thomas Curtis was on the snow *Elizabeth*, bound for St. John's Island.

Curtis found the voyage to be something of an education.

Lesson 1 — The effects of seasickness on servants: "My man Harry... certainly was very sick, and as he laid & puked, the vessel rolled him in it, so that he was a drole figure. His only request was, that the vessel would lay still one minute & he should be well." And this just a day out of London. *Elizabeth* never did lay still enough for Harry, and he jumped ship half-way down the Thames.

Lesson 2 — Sharing your booze with the sailors: "We gave some rum to the sailors which made them a little Tipsy for which I was very sorry for Afterwards, for if a gale of Wind had happen[d] to come on we might have all been lost. I mention this as a Caution to Others and we never did the like again."

Lesson 3 — The medicinal qualities of salt water: " I found it to be a good phisick. Several mornings I drank half a pint and found it a Suitable Quantity — Others drank more. I have seen some of the men drink a Quart. Then it always operated powerfully upwards and downwards."

All in all, the voyage out was unremarkable. Boredom was relieved by a poop deck donnybrook between one of the Stewart boys and a passenger from steerage. Stewart won when his opponent "beat his head by Accident against the Fleuk of the Anchor." Additional entertainment was provided by the mid-ocean rescue of the ship's pig, who had fallen overboard. But as the *Elizabeth* neared St. John's Island it was caught in an autumn gale. Life then got very interesting indeed.

The storm battered the tiny snow for three days, driving it closer and closer to the sandbars of Malpeque Bay. In desperation, the captain ordered the masts cut down and threw out the largest anchor he had. "With the masts overboard, there being nothing to steady her," Curtis recalled, "its impossible to describe how she rowl[d] about — the Sea breaking over like to wash us off." But the wind continued to push the helpless *Elizabeth* closer to shore, tearing away her anchors one by one. As the last anchor was played out, the Captain suggested they try to make a run over the sandbars to the quieter water closer to shore. As soon as the tide reached its peak, he ordered the anchor cable cut, and *Elizabeth* began her run to shore.

Curtis remembers hitting, then clearing, no fewer than four sandbars. Unfortunately there were five sandbars between the *Elizabeth* and safety. After a gallant run she fetched up about a hundred yards from shore. But that was close enough for the ship's boats to ferry passengers and crew ashore. The only fatality was the ship's pig.

It was not exactly the arrival Curtis had been hoping for.

Most of his gear — his guns, his powder, his tools, his four dozen shirts — was lost on the *Elizabeth*. Worse still, it was November and it was cold. "Notwithstanding our Blessings," he wrote, "we whare still in want of many things to make us comfortable — no chair no Table no bed Nothing to Eat no house to cover us."

One morning I went in the Woods to kill some partridges....

After a few hungry, wet, uncomfortable days camping out on the sand dunes,[3] the castaways were led to civilization. Curtis was not impressed. "We soon came in sight of a house. I thought it had been a cow house or a place for cattle but was inform'd it was a Dwelling house." His first impression of fabled New London — a clutch of log huts huddled in the woods — wasn't much better. "I was mutch Surprized to see what a place it was, It being so very different from the Idea I had formed of it. I then began to repent of my Voyage and wish my Selfe in Old London again, but wishes and repentance was now too late." Winter was coming, and no boats would be putting into the Colony until the next spring.

Curtis decided to make the best of a bad situation. He found a place to stay and was able to salvage one of his firearms. At least there would be time to do some hunting — even though there seemed to be an unusual amount of snow on the ground. "One morning I took my Gun and went in the Woods to kill some partridges if I could find any. I had not gone far before I trod on the Crown of a great tree and Sunk as if I gone in a Well about 15 or 16 feet. Endeavouring to get out again by taking hold or treading on the boughs it brought sutch large quantity's of snow on my head as Allmost to Smother me.... This I thought was the worst sport I ever met with."

Disappointed as a hunter, he was also convinced the prospects for plying his trade as a sawyer were not promising. "In a Country where the snow is ten or twelve feet deep on a level in the woods it is not an easy matter to convey large Trees.... I was informed allso It is impossible for Men to work in the Woods in Summer — the Musketoes would soon blind them, and many other stinging flys that's very troublesome."

But the worst thing of all was the cold. Proponents for the Colony preached that the arctic winters were actually beneficial. Although more severe, it was a drier, more *bracing* cold than the clammy dampness of Mother England. They must have lived in tighter houses than Curtis'. He certainly didn't buy the concept that Island winters were good for the health.

"I had on occasion one morning to go to Joseph Rooke, who live in part of the same house as I. He was in bed and fast asleep. I saw on the Blankett a large fleak of Ice that reach[d] from his mouth as near as I could gues about 16 or 18 inches long."

---

[3] "I was Sorry to find the Sow that was in the Vessel was Drowned for if a live it might have been very Servisabl."

Later that winter he and some companions made a trip back to the *Elizabeth* wreck to see if anything more might be salvaged. They were able to raise several casks of salt pork and flour — some of it even edible. But while returning to a nearby settlement, Curtis almost froze to death. All but fainting from the cold, when he took his boots off he discovered "My feet and all was freez^d together. My toes was as hard as a board though not painful. Fortunate for me G Hardy now comes in And being Acquainted with my Situation, Ordered in a small tub of Water cold in which he said I must confine my feet 5 Hours or Else they would rot off. ... For the first 4 or 5 days my feet was amazingly Swell^d. I thought it was like a violent Gout for I could not refrain crying out if touch^d by a feather....This with many other Instances of Severyty in the Climate convinced me that this Island was not agreeable to an English constitution."

By springtime Curtis had had enough.

"I may now say I have been on this well recommended Island about six months and had not seen the colour of the land.... I suffer^d so mutch this Winter I determin^d to go the First Opportunity." Despite the danger from American privateers he took passage on the first vessel that came into the bay. "I cant express The Joy I Felt when I got to my Native Country the 2nd of Feb. 1777." Thomas the Adventurer had come home.

Twice a year he would play his pipes to drive away the rats.

P. John Burden

A Dance Called America

...we performed a dance which I suppose the Emigration from Skye has occasioned. They call it "America." A brisk reel is played...and goes on till all are set in motion, setting and wheeling round each other. It shows how emigration catches on till all are set afloat.... Mrs. MacKinnon told me that when last year the ship sailed from Portree for America the people onshore were almost distracted when they saw their relations go off; they lay down on the ground and tumbled and tore the grass with their teeth. This year there was not a tear shed. The people on shore seem to think they will soon follow.

—James Boswell, A Tour of the Highlands, 1773

ome time ago, I was called on to settle an argument. "What's the most common surname on the Island," the question began, "Gallant or MacDonald?" (Now that the fixed link makes it possible to actually *stray* onto the Island, this is a valuable hint to lost Come-from-awayers. If you come across two people arguing over things like this, you're on Prince Edward Island.) Anyway. I whipped out a ruler and a current phone book and I solved that puzzle by calculating the MacDonalds and Gallants centimetre by centimetre. The MacDonalds won: 550 cm to 440 cm. (Who says historians don't live full and active lives?) Thus, by the most scientific of methods, we come to the topic of the Scots on Prince Edward Island.

America now begins to dawn very near out here. We begin now to think no more of it than formerly a jaunt. We begin to look upon America as but one of our islands on the coast, and on the sea that intervenes as but a little brook.... You know, there was a time when people thought the first emigrants a set of madmen, but, it seems this craze has been very prolific and continuing. I doe believe that in a few years there will be none remaining of the old residents on this coast.

—Augustus MacDonald, writing his sister Helen in Tracadie, 1801

The Scots dominated the early settlement of the colony. Over our first fifty years as a British possession, around two-thirds of the settlers arriving hailed from Scotland. By 1900, half the population considered itself Scottish. As late as 1960 — the last time census takers asked such impertinent questions — one Islander in three claimed mainly Scottish ancestry. We are the most "Scottish" jurisdiction — state, province, etc. — outside Scotland itself.

The Island's major era of settlement was between 1770 and 1840. By coincidence, this was also the best time in history for getting out of Scotland. Political repression, economic catastrophe, social chaos. Scotland — especially the Highlands — was a case study of a society turned on its ear. Some estimate that as much as a quarter of the population fled the country in these years.

> *From and after the First Day of August, 1747, no Man or Boy, within that part of Great Britain called Scotland, other than such as shall be employed as officers and soldiers in His Majestey's Forces, shall, on any pretence whatsoever, wear or put on the clothes commonly called Highland Clothes (that is to say) the Plaid, Philiebeg or little kilt, Trowse, Shoulder Belts or any part whatsoever of what peculiarily belongs to the Highland Garb, and that no Tartan, or parti-coloured plaid or stuff shall be used for Great Coats, or for Upper Coats...*

> —Amendment to the Disarming Act of 1715

In addition to outlawing kilts and tartan, the Disarming Acts also made it illegal to play the bagpipes and discouraged the speaking of the Gaelic. In short, they were designed to destroy Highland culture. In retrospect, they hardly seem necessary. The Clans themselves were doing a fine job of destroying their own culture. Clan Chieftains discovered sheep could generate far more profit than people. With fewer arguments. Since the thin soil of the Highlands couldn't support both sheep and people, the people had to go. The sheep farmers, observed a pessimistic John MacDonald in 1785,

> *are getting into Knoydart and to the neighbourhood of Glenfinnan, so that farms, which formerly have supported 15 families, have now only 4 or 5 grey plaited shepherds, and as many thousand sheep. — Cows and men will in 40 years be as rare to be seen as Deer in that ill-fated country.*

> —John MacDonald to his brother Donald, 1785

Conditions were not so grim in the Lowlands, but even there the Industrial and Agricultural revolutions threw many out of traditional lands and occupations. Though their exodus was not as romantic, they also came to the Island by the thousands. In 1775, in what must rank as one of the world's first opinion surveys, Island-bound emigrants aboard the *Lovely Nelly* were asked why they were leaving Scotland. The replies:

> To seek better bread than he can get here.
> To provide for his family a better livelihood.
> To mend himself.
> To better himself.
> To mend his fortune.
> To get a place. [from a schoolteacher]
> Could not with all his industry support his family.

> *I live better than I ever did in Scotland off Tea and Sugar, Beef Mutton and Pork and Rum three times in the day.*

> —Alexander Stewart, writing to his parents in Scotland, 1805

The Island's disproportionate Scots population is mainly due to the Highlanders. Where Lowlanders tended to emigrate as individuals or single families, Highlanders were more comfortable in larger groups. As Dr. Johnson noted in 1773...

> *...whole neighbourhoods form parties for removal: so that departure from their native country is no longer exile... They sit down in a better climate, surrounded by their kindred and friends; they carry with them their language, their opinions, their popular songs, and hereditary merriment; they change nothing but their place of abode.*

> —Samuel Johnson, *Journey to the Western Isles*, 1773

It was like a siphon. Once a node of Highland settlement was in place on the Island, it naturally attracted more Highlanders to the Colony. This in turn seemed to reinforce their sense of community identity.

> *The settlers... retain many of the habits and superstitions that were formerly so prevalent in their native country... indeed, it is not a little remarkable that many of the ancient and traditionary stories, now passing away and nearly forgotten in England, Ireland and Scotland, are religiously remembered and preserved in our colonies.*

> —R. Montgomery Martin, *History of Nova Scotia, Cape Breton, The Sable Islands, Prince Edward Island, the Bermudas, Newfoundland, etc.,etc.*, 1837

In some ways, Highland culture fared better here than in the home country. By 1830, for instance, there were twice as many Highland Catholics on Prince Edward Island as there were in the Highlands. Gaelic was the second most common language. So many fiddlers emigrated that the tradition almost disappeared in the Scottish countryside. In 1790, officials in Scotland estimated that one person in ten could play the fiddle. Fifty years later, the Scottish countryside had succumbed to a ghastly fate. There, by the mid-1800s, the accordion was acknowledged as the folk instrument of choice.

And then there were the pipes. Andrew Macphail remembered the pipes from his childhood in Orwell:

> The mill... was leased to a man called Malcolm Gillis. He played the bagpipes, and wore a scotch bonnet for the ceremonial. He would not play without that emblem. Twice a year he would play his pipes in the dairy to drive away the rats. It was long before we learned that music was a thing to be enjoyed for itself and not for any ulterior purpose. Such as freedom from rats.
>
> — Sir Andrew Macphail, *The Master's Wife*, 1939

Kilts, tartan, Gaelic and bagpipes — so much of the Scots' popular image revolves around the culture and trappings of the Highlands, it's easy to lose sight of the Lowlanders. Their language was English, their religion mainly Protestant. They had no "exotic garb" or quaint customs to set them apart. Their legacy to the Island's culture is harder to trace.

Lowlanders were known for their profound respect for education. Even the poorest citizens had to be literate — how else could they read their Bibles? Literacy was almost universal in the Lowlands. Even in the relatively "backward" Highlands, the literacy rate was over fifty per cent. Given this heritage, it is no surprise that Prince Edward Island had one of the first Free Education Acts in North America.

> The Scotchman, habituated to greater privations in his native country, has probably left it with the full determination of undergoing any hardships that may lead to the acquisition of solid advantages; he acts with great caution and industry, subjects himself to many inconveniences, neglects the comforts for some time... and in time certainly succeeds in surmounting all difficulties; and then, and not till then, does he willingly enjoy the comforts of life.
>
> —James MacGregor, *Historical and Descriptive Sketches*, 1832

Another mark they left was on the land. Lowlanders were known as the pre-eminent farmers of Europe. "Scientific Farming," pioneered in the Lowlands in the early 1800s, sparked an agricultural revolution every bit as significant as the Industrial Revolution. Emigrants trained in Lowland farming methods were held in particular esteem:

> no settlers are prized more, and few so much, upon that Island, as settlers from Dumfries-shire and the southern counties of Scotland. None excel them in agricultural knowledge, domestic energy, or steady, industrious habits.
>
> —Walter Johnstone, *Letters and Travels*, 1822

Although some of what the Scots brought to the Island has faded away — the Gaelic, for instance, is long gone — their legacy is a rich one. It goes deeper than tartans and bagpipes, kilts and ceilidhs. Their heritage is so firmly woven into the fabric of Island culture that the cloth would not be recognizable without them.

This is the isle of contentment
where we are now.
Our seed is fruitful here;
oats grow
and wheat, in full bloom,
turnip, cabbage and peas.
Sugar from trees
may be had for free;
we have it in large chunks.
There is fresh red rum
in every dwelling and shop,
abundant as the stream,
being imbibed here.

—translated from a Gaelic ballad composed by Malcolm Ban Buchanan, on his emigration to Orwell, 1803.

Chieftain to Capitalist

Part One: The Chieftain

The chiefs now being deprived of their jurisdiction have already lost much of their influence, and as they gradually degenerate from patriarchal rulers to rapacious landlords, they will divest themselves of the little that remains.

— Samuel Johnson, *Journey to the Western Isles*, 1773

ohn MacDonald was born in the Highlands of Scotland in 1742. He had a privileged upbringing. Educated in Germany, fluent in seven languages, he was "one of the most finished and accomplished young gentlemen of his generation." The Glenaladale MacDonalds were an important branch of the MacDonald clan. Even though the Clan had picked the losing side in the famous Rebellion of 1745, it was still a significant force in Scotland. As heir to the Glenaladale estate, John MacDonald was destined to be a fairly powerful and respected man. Despite this, he was not happy with the future he saw for himself or his country.

Scared silly by the failed 1745 Rebellion, the English had passed a series of laws designed to crush the Highlands. Being Catholic, speaking Gaelic, playing the bagpipes, wearing a kilt — all of these were technically illegal in John MacDonald's youth. Although these strictures had eased by the 1760s, the Highlands were still smarting.

In addition to political persecution, the Highlands' way of life was failing before the twin assault of overpopulation and economic hardship. Worse still, MacDonald's betters in the Clan hierarchy were beginning to see their kin, "the people," as little more than a resource that supported an increasingly luxurious lifestyle.

Men of MacDonald's rank — once responsible for rallying the Clan to the Chieftain's battle standard — were becoming little more than estate agents whose job was to wring as much out of the tenantry as they could. Disgusted with the present, and fearful for the future, John MacDonald began to look "for a feasible method of leaving the inhospitable part of the world which has fallen our share." If the Highlands had become hostile to the traditional ways, perhaps they could be transplanted to a better part of the world. In 1772 he scraped together enough money to buy Lot 36, and bundled 210 settlers onto a hired boat called the *Alexander*. A year later he wrapped up his affairs in Scotland and followed. Their new home was to be a place the French had named Tracadie.

The British had designed the Island to be a self-supporting colony. To perform to specifications, it needed settlers — thousands of them — arriving every year. According to the theory, settlers would clear the land and build the farms to raise the crops to pay the rents to allow the proprietors to pay the taxes that would pay the salaries of the colony's civil "infrastructure." Until these settlers arrived, the colony was as fragile as a house of cards. At first, settlers came by dozens, not thousands. But by the early 1770s they were at least arriving by the hundreds, and the investment of influential people like John MacDonald was taken as a vote of confidence in the colony's future.

Then the Crown's more mature colonies to the south rose in rebellion, demanding independence. The Americans' revolution was a disaster for the Island. The uncertainty it brought slowed emigration to a trickle and put a crimp in everybody's development plans.

Strapped for cash, MacDonald took a Captain's commission in the Royal Highland Emigrants in 1775 and spent the next eight years fighting the rebels. Though he never saw battle, he served gallantly as a staff officer in Halifax. At the war's end in 1783 he came back to his estate, only to find an even longer fight in the offing.

When MacDonald went off to the war, he left Tracadie in the charge of his sister Helen. Given the magnitude of the task and the tenor of the times, Helen MacDonald did a magnificent job. Under her leadership, "the people" carved farmsteads out of wilderness. Before they emigrated, "the people" had probably never even seen trees, let alone forests. Helen guided them in an era when the law considered women the property of their kin. There were, though, a few problems that proved too much for even her capable hands.

The first was with Governor Patterson. Patterson, you recall, was the colony's first Governor who, after not being paid for ten years, decided to take land in lieu of back salary. Even after learning that his own land was spared, MacDonald was disturbed by Patterson's methods. Captain John came home in a fighting mood. He had just lost one war. He had no intention of losing another. Walter Patterson would have to go.

The battle took place in London. MacDonald mobilized his fellow proprietors, among whom were some very prominent individuals. Pointing to his own service in the recent war, he painted Patterson as a rascal who stole land from loyal Britons as they fought to defend their King. Though Patterson soon arrived to tell his own side of the story, MacDonald's arguments had a more powerful impact. The Governor was sacked, then instructed to return the land he'd seized. His victory over the troublesome Patterson complete, MacDonald returned to Tracadie for good in 1792. After twenty years of warring, he may have been looking forward to some peace and quiet.

It was not to be.

Sticky-fingered governors were to be the least of the MacDonalds' problems, as it turned out. "The People" were no longer playing by the old rules. Some of the settlers drifted onto adjacent estates, where they could "squat" on land for free. Others simply refused to give the instant loyalty and obedience due the clan chief back home, where life was land and land was scarce. After two decades of warring with Americans and administrators, John MacDonald rounded out his life quarrelling with his kinsmen. "I wish not to be squabbling with them," he despaired, "I wish to be on a pleasant footing with them... but they will never give the tenth part of that Justice due to me which they will readily and without grudge show to others."

John MacDonald tried to plant the ancient and venerable clan system in the New World. Toward the end of his life he conceded the seeds weren't taking like he thought they might. Something unintended was growing.

His son Donald would find out what kind of fruit would be borne.

Chieftain to Capitalist

Part Two: The Proprietor

Born to Captain John and his wife Margaret in 1795, Donald McDonald had wealth, position and a good education. Lord of a fifteen-thousand-acre estate, he was master to hundreds of tenants — many of them his kin. According to tradition, they owed him respect, loyalty and obedience. How then did he become, if not the most hated, then certainly the most shot-at landlord of his era?

Part of Donald's problems had roots back in the Highlands. There, when he was still a young man, many of the evils his father had feared came to pass. The ancient culture based on clan loyalties, which the English had tried and failed to crush, was finally destroyed by the clan chiefs themselves. Some of the more greedy chieftains realized they could make more money from their lands by renting it to sheep instead of people. Blood ties or no, the people had to go. Thousands were evicted as their leaseholds were cleared to make sheep pasture. Even the more soft-hearted clan lords joined in this gold rush, inflicting more hardship on their helpless kinsmen than the hated English ever had.

Settlers in the colonies, even dirt-poor tenant farmers, maintained a surprising level of communication with their homeland. Stories about the treatment of the Highlanders were soon filtering onto the Island. Donald McDonald was the highest-ranking clan chief in the Colony. Indeed, now that the trappings of Highland culture had become very fashionable, he revelled in the role. But it was natural that some of the resentment generated by "The Clearances" would fall on him.[1] Especially given his personality.

It would not appear that Donald was an easy man to love. He was, by most accounts, a hard, arrogant man with a quick temper and not much charity in his soul. He gained a reputation for giving short leases and quick eviction notices. Even his fellow proprietors found him hard to get along with.

The final factor was the political climate on the Island. The first settlers who came to the Colony had been grateful to get such fine farm-

---

[1] In addition to this, many of Donald's tenants were Irish, who just plain resented landlords, no matter what their background.

One afternoon McDonald was on his way to Charlottetown.

land for such low rents. All they had to do was chop down the trees. Hard work, granted, but their situations seemed enviable, compared to those they had left. But subsequent generations adopted New World standards of measurement. They looked to other colonies or to the United States, where settlers could *buy* land,[2] almost as good, for virtually nothing. Suddenly their situation didn't seem as enviable, and they began to agitate for political change and land reform. John MacDonald had despaired at how his tenants squabbled amongst each other and wouldn't show him proper respect and obedience. Donald's tenants began to question his very right to be their landlord.

In the 1830s McDonald became a favoured target of the Escheat party. He fought back from his own position in the Legislature. In the 1840s it appeared that he had won, when the Escheat party disintegrated after London refused to listen to their program of reform. But, denied a political avenue to air their grievances, some of his tenants declared open warfare.

In the summer of 1850, arsonists destroyed a cottage and some

---

[2] Heckfire. In some jurisdictions, they were actually *giving* the stuff away!

barns on the estate at Glenaladale. McDonald responded by hiring armed guards to protect his property. Three weeks later one of these guards spotted him standing at his own back door, took him for an intruder and let fly with a shotgun. As he recovered from buckshot wounds to his head, arm and legs, McDonald apparently decided he could better defend himself, and dismissed the guards.

Though relations with the tenantry continued to deteriorate, things were quiet until the following July. One afternoon McDonald was on his way to Charlottetown. As he got to the end of his lane, gunmen on both sides of the road opened fire. He fell, bleeding profusely, as his assailants made their escape. Some time passed before one of his tenants came upon him. The tenant looked — and kept on going. This happened several more times in the ensuing hours before someone took pity, bundled him into a cart and took him to a doctor in Charlottetown. Legend has it that the good Samaritan had his house burned for his troubles.

The community was shocked, but not entirely sympathetic.

The Governor, that bastion of landholders' rights, suggested the tale might have been exaggerated, and also that McDonald may have brought the attack on himself. Although a reward of £100 was offered, no one was ever caught. To add insult to his injuries, the following spring McDonald himself was convicted of an assault on one of his tenants.

Enough was enough. While visiting his sons, who had set up a profitable business in Montreal, McDonald decided to sell his estate on the Island and move permanently to the more hospitable Lower Canada. I hope the decision finally brought contentment to an angry soul, for within a week he was dead. The body that had withstood repeated buckshot and bullet wounds proved no match for the cholera epidemic that swept through Montreal that summer. A final irony? The cholera that killed Donald McDonald was brought to Montreal by Irish tenant farmers who were fleeing their own landlords.

Chieftain to Capitalist

Part Three: The Capitalist

It couldn't have been easy, growing up in Donald McDonald's household. Aside from the sporadic gunfire, there is no indication that Donald was any more yielding to his children than he was to his tenants. Born in 1831, William Christopher discovered this as a teenager. You see, Donald had decided that William C. would be a priest. But William C. didn't take to his pre-priestly training. At sixteen he announced to his father he'd have nothing more to do with that career path.[3] A wrathful father punished his willful son by throwing him into the barely-respectable world of business. An apprenticeship agreement was struck with Daniel Brennan, a local merchant and distant cousin. William C. was given a stipend of £15 per year and all the groceries he could deliver.

William's course in business training lasted less than a year.

One morning he had an argument with Brennan over the finer points of a particular transaction. The argument grew heated. Brennan settled the matter by deducting a portion of young Macdonald's wages. That afternoon, while Brennan was absent, William C. re-deducted his pay from the till, packed a bag and boarded the boat for Boston.

Living in Boston was his brother Augustus, who had already fled the family estate. Augustus got William a job as a clerk in the firm he worked for. Soon the brothers were dabbling in transactions on their own account. In the early 1850s the Macdonald brothers relocated to Montreal and set up a business of their own. At first they dealt in whale oil and other smelly things that burned. A few years later they began to specialize in another smelly, combustible commodity — tobacco.

If you've ever seen a pack of Export "A" cigarettes, or run across the huge corporation that still bears his name, you've encountered William Christopher Macdonald. Legend suggests he couldn't abide the

---

[3] Indeed, though he never explained why, the experience seemed to leave William C. with an abiding dislike for the Catholic Church. Years later, after he'd become obscenely wealthy, he gave large donations to Protestant Prince of Wales College while completely ignoring Catholic St. Dunstan's. It may have been no more than an homage to his Anglican mother, Matilda Brecken, and a final swipe at his overbearing father.

smell of tobacco and forbade smoking in his presence. This didn't stop him from making a huge fortune from the stuff. By the 1860s his tobacco company was one of the most successful in the Canadas. By the 1870s he was one of the richest individuals in the country.

His father and grandfather were legendary for their tempers and the battles they got into. Although William Christopher was also regarded as a "grim and crotchety old man," he was remembered for his generosity. He made sure that every one of his nieces and nephews got the formal education he'd been denied. He was also determined to maintain the family in the style to which they'd become accustomed.[4] To this end he commissioned a magnificent house for his brother John on the Tracadie estate. William himself rarely visited. He much preferred Montreal.

He was best known for his public philanthropy. Over the years $6 million went to various parts of McGill University. Another $5 million founded Macdonald College, one of the country's leading agricultural schools. On the Island, his charities financed a new wing for Prince of Wales College and for many years supported the province's first consolidated school system.

"You must exert yourself and push on," he once lectured one of his brothers. "Let nothing stop you. If you must lose all, stop not to grieve — it is unbecoming in a man, as well as useless — stop only to plan, continue and devise means to meet your ends. Let your aim next to heaven be *superiority*."

William Christopher died in 1917. With him passed the main line of the Glenaladale MacDonalds on Prince Edward Island. In 1780, John MacDonald left Scotland because he felt capitalism was destroying the Highland way of life. By giving his people a new start in the New World, he hoped he could maintain the old ways of kinship and clan loyalty. The success of the latter dream is best judged by the career of his son Donald — the most shot-at landlord in Island history. In a final irony, the family is probably best known for the exploits of grandson William — one of the most successful capitalists in Canadian history.

[A note on spelling — the various versions of "MacDonald" that appear are not the whim of the author. Each generation settled on a different spelling. Captain John was a "MacDonald." His son Donald preferred "McDonald." His grandson adopted "Macdonald."]

---

[4] At least as long as they didn't cross him. Then he'd cut them off cold.

Hellfire Jack

It is commonly said, there has been no peace on the Island since the Stewart family arrived on it, and there will be no peace on it, while they are employed in public offices on it.

— John MacDonald of Tracadie

he night of November 6, 1775, might have been a hard one for the snow[1] *Elizabeth*, but it was a good one for Island history. As you remember, the *Elizabeth* brought Thomas Curtis to the Island, and its crash landing on the sandbars of Malpeque Bay was the start of a winter he might have preferred to forget. (But didn't, and wrote about in wonderful detail.)

Another passenger on board for the *Elizabeth's* final landfall was John Stewart, who came to be known as "Hellfire Jack." Unlike Curtis, Jack Stewart's adventure on the Island was to last much longer than one winter.

John Stewart came here as the teenage son of Peter Stewart, the colony's second chief justice. The title was a grand one, but the family was aware that the colony's first chief justice, the late John Duport, had not been able to draw a penny of salary over five years of service. It was said that his wife, Jane, died of starvation. The Stewart family knew life in the New World might include the occasional struggle.

Jack Stewart was well suited for the rough-and-tumble society he'd just moved to. If he'd died young, Hellfire Jack would be best remembered for his temper. The sight of him picking, or trying to pick, fights with fellow

---

[1] You may have been wondering since Chapter 5 what the crank a *snow* is. A snow was a two-masted vessel, rigged very much like a brig. Very popular in the 1700s, the rig for some reason fell out of favour by the mid-1800s. If you already knew this information, then this entire footnote has been an utter waste of time, and I apologize. My editor made me do it.

members of the colonial elite was a fairly regular one on the streets of Charlottetown. The card for one memorable battle in 1784 included the Colony's ranking judge and its provost marshal. But for a sudden rush of sanity it also would have included the Colony's chief Anglican priest.

Over the years, Hellfire Jack shed some of his temper and gained an estate. The estate had its heart near the head of the Hillsborough

His career as a political intriguer was just coming into blossom.

River, and the village that grew there still bears Stewart's name. Unfortunately, the estate also bordered on Tracadie, home and headquarters to John MacDonald. Captain John. Laird of the Glenaladale settlers. Probably the second most volatile temper in the colony. The fact these two shared a boundary was bound to bring conflict. It did. On a winter day in 1798, the feud came to a head.

Picture if you will. It is a bitterly cold day. MacDonald is trundling down the street, wadded up in two watch coats, and a variety of scarves, muffs and mittens. He encounters Stewart, his enemy, who begins to harangue him. A shouting match develops. Finally, the Glenaladale can take no more, and whips out his dirk. At this point he realizes he has made several errors. He is fifty-six — Stewart, barely forty. He is wearing so many clothes he can hardly move. Finally, and perhaps most vitally, he is wielding a dirk. Stewart is equipped with a broadsword. "I would have been unable to withstand the pressure from his prodigious cut-and-thrust sword," MacDonald later recalled, "had his sword arm not trembled." For possibly the first time in his life, Jack Stewart backed down from a fight. His refusal to impale his neighbour seemed to bring his career as a brawler to an end. His career as a political intriguer was just coming into blossom.

Jack Stewart lived under six different governors. He loathed three of them. His hatred of the first, Governor Patterson, was natural. Patterson wronged the Stewart clan on two occasions. In the mid-1780s he engaged in a not-too-secret affair with Stewart's stepmother, heaping great embarrassment on the family. What was worse, Patterson failed to cut the Stewarts in on a sufficient share of the loot when he tried to steal a third of the colony for himself and his cronies.

Stewart got along much better with Edmund Fanning, Patterson's successor, and for the next twenty years Stewart and his brother Charles quietly collected offices and prospered.

But administrations change, and Fanning's successor, J. F. W. DesBarres, ran afoul of Jack Stewart's good graces. Toward the end of the Fanning regime Stewart had secured a re-survey of the boundary between his estate and John MacDonald's. As the re-survey was executed by a Stewart brother-in-law, no one was much surprised when it announced that several hundred acres of the MacDonald estate actually belonged to Jack Stewart! Unfortunately, the new governor was a mapmaker of international reputation, and when he rejected the results, he gained a lifelong enemy. Stewart began to spread the rumour that the new Governor was interested in — horror of horrors — land reform! It took the better part of eight years, but by 1812 Stewart managed to secure DesBarres' recall.

You wonder how long it took, after DesBarres' successor arrived, for Jack Stewart and his cronies to curse themselves for arranging his downfall. The new Governor was Charles Douglass Smith. His brother Sydney was a famous admiral. Charles himself would claim a small portion of history. He would be remembered as the worst chief executive the small but put-upon colony of Prince Edward Island ever had to endure.

Thus it was, at an age when others might have been looking forward to a quiet retirement, Jack Stewart found himself in the last and most important fight of his life. This fight climaxed in 1823 in Charlottetown when a meeting to enumerate the Governor's faults resulted in thirty pages of petition demanding his removal. Stewart was delegated to deliver the petition to Halifax.

When he caught wind of the petition, the Governor decided that the resolutions were libellous or treasonous or both, and sent troops to arrest Stewart. They chased him through Charlottetown. They chased him through Mount Stewart. They lost him on the docks where, legend has it, he hid in a turnip barrel (or possibly a rum puncheon) bound for Nova Scotia. The petition was delivered. The evil governor was recalled. A few months later, Hellfire Jack came home with a new governor at his side. It was a fitting capstone to an unusually colourful career.

Stewart became something of a collector in his "declining" years. He collected civil service positions — a favourite hobby for the Island's ruling class — and titles from a grateful Legislature. Retired to his estate at Mount Stewart, he made frequent processions downriver to Charlottetown in his personal longboat. With a piper in the bow and crew decked out in Highland costume, it must have been quite an aristocratic sight.

Unfortunately, the record's final glimpse of Jack Stewart is not a happy one. As he neared his mid-seventies, his mind wandered into insanity. In the spring of 1834, a court declared he was incapable of running his own affairs. Indeed, it appeared he hadn't enjoyed a lucid interval for the better part of a year. Two months later Hellfire Jack, Scourge of Governors and Terror to his Peers, died from "a surfeit of fat meat."

"Have Altar, Will Travel"

The good Scottish people seem sincere in their religion, strongly attached to their pastors, and as demonstrative in their piety as the Irish. During Mass you hear them sighing, and at the elevation they burst into sobs. Many of them keep joining and separating their hands while they pray, and their arms are in continual motion during Holy Sacrifice. Others strike their breasts with great force. Still others remain prostrate with their face to the floor all through the Mass.

— Bishop Joseph Octave Plessis, on visiting
Prince Edward Island, 1812

The 1750s weren't the best of times to be born a Catholic in the Highlands of Scotland. Officially proscribed throughout the Empire, Catholicism was especially frowned upon in the Highlands, where it was identified with resistance to British rule. Although the harsher measures — taken after the failed rebellion of 1745 — were fading into memory, official policy was still to harass those who were determined to worship in an unauthorized religion. Despite this, thousands remained faithful to the Church they'd been born into. The Church that Angus Bernard MacEachern was born into in 1759.

The son of Hugh Ban MacEachern and Mary MacDonald, Angus was born near a place called Kinlochmoidart, part of the Glenaladale MacDonald estate in the western Highlands. His priestly potential was recognized when he was a boy. In 1772 his family decided to join the Glenaladale emigration to St. John's Island. Hugh MacDonald, Bishop for the Highlands, encouraged the thirteen-year-old Angus to stay behind and study for the priesthood. He entered the secret Catholic college at Buorblach. (The key to Buorblach's security was probably the fact no Englishman could pronounce it well enough to ask where it was.) After Buorblach he was off to the Royal Scots College in Vallalolid, Spain. He was ordained in 1787.

Church authorities were encouraged by the promise of Bishop MacDonald's protégé. Since priests were desperately needed in the Highlands, they sent the competent Gaelic-speaking MacEachern back to Scotland. But Father MacEachern missed his family, and asked for a posting on St. John's Island. Assignment as a missionary on the Inner Hebrides may have contributed to his longing. Lucky for him, there was also a desperate shortage of priests in the New World. In 1790, with extreme reluctance, his superiors in Scotland allowed him to emigrate.

His new boss was the Bishop of Quebec.

Responsible for all of British North America, the Bishop had lots of work for the new priest. St. John's Island had been without a pastor since 1785, when the last one died. The parishioners were mainly Acadians and Highlanders — the poorest people in the Colony. They didn't possess a single church and, living on the fringe of the Diocese, were easy to overlook. Father MacEachern would be the only priest in the Colony. The Bishop, on discovering his fluency in Gaelic, decided to give him Cape Breton and northern Nova Scotia to look after as well.

The sheer size of his parish was the most daunting part of MacEachern's job. The best roads were little more than paths through the woods. The easiest way to get about was by water. In summer he hired a canoe, or hitched rides on the small trading vessels that kept the Maritime colonies in contact with each other. For winter travel he designed an ingenious portable altar. Housed in a small boat with sleigh runners, it was light enough to pull by hand, and seaworthy enough to float across the occasional stretch of open water. The sight of Father MacEachern hauling his portable church down the colony's frozen rivers became a common one.

The many hundreds of solitary miles MacEachern trudged probably contributed to an extremely well-developed sense of patience. This he needed. His flock — especially the Scottish lambs — were considered a rough-and-ready bunch, even by frontier standards. "Before and after Mass," reported one fastidious observer, "they were in the habit of talking as freely as they would in a profane place. They also allowed their dogs to enter the church and run around as if they were in the houses of their masters." Even more scandalous was "the immodesty of

For winter travel he designed an ingenious portable altar.

P. John Burden

the women, who came to the sacraments with their throats exposed to a degree that should not allow them even to enter the church."

Father MacEachern's patience could also be tested by the more refined members of the parish. In the early 1800s, he came to logger-heads with the most powerful Catholic in the colony — John MacDonald, Laird of Tracadie.

Captain John had a practical, no-nonsense attitude toward his religion. "I do not wish you to be a weak, credulous, foolish or ridiculous devotee," he once scolded his daughter. "It is very well for those who have nothing else to do to be constantly at their prayers, or to make very long prayers; but those who have other work and duties upon hand, must only give a reasonable time to their prayers, in order to perform their duties." Part of MacDonald's duty, as he saw it, was to point out the basic flaws in MacEachern's plan to build the Island's first Catholic church at St. Andrews.

It was far too extravagant a building for such a poor parish, MacDonald complained. Besides, it was in entirely the wrong location. St. Andrews might be a convenient spot for Father MacEachern, but it was miles from Tracadie, where Captain John lived, and where the church should have been in the first place. The Glenaladale declared he would not set foot in the place. He instructed his tenants to do the same.

MacEachern countered with a tactic few of Captain John's secular opponents could afford — he ignored him. The church was built. The congregation attended. In 1810 MacDonald died. Problem solved.

In 1813 the new Governor, C. D. Smith, provided a more chal-lenging test. Smith was dismayed at the number of Catholics in the colony, and the relative ease with which they led their lives. Catholi-cism was supposed to be a proscribed religion. It was a Governor's duty to harass them! Smith ordered that the Catholic officials in his govern-ment be dismissed and decreed that no marriage conducted by a Catho-lic priest would be legally registered.

Father MacEachern was furious. He wrote that he'd rather send his people to Nova Scotia to be married than submit to "a penny paper of such obnoxious dye." But he refrained from a public outburst. In-stead, in a fascinating demonstration of how the Colonial power struc-ture worked, he complained to his superior, the Bishop of Quebec. The Bishop had a quiet word with the Governor-in-Chief — Smith's su-perior. Smith in turn was instructed to stop making trouble for the Colo-ny's Catholics. To MacEachern's credit, he resisted the temptation to celebrate his victory, and a few years later was one of the few on the Island able to claim to be on good terms with Governor Smith.

Ironically, his longest and most difficult struggle was with his superiors in Quebec. The Island was an easy parish to overlook, and MacEachern fought continually for more resources — especially more priests to ease the workload. In 1819, partly as punishment, partly as a bribe, he was made titular Bishop of Rosen, with responsibility for New Brunswick, Prince Edward Island and the Magdalen Islands. Later, as an afterthought, Cape Breton was added to the charge. Titular bishop means you get the title, but none of the authority and resources to go with it. At first he applied the same quiet patience that had won previous battles, but in later years his disgust with his superiors grew more vocal. "Altho' money is as plenty with them as figs in Rome," he wrote a colleague, "I never received one shilling for my travelling expenses."

As he got older, MacEachern's most pressing worry became who would look after the parish when he was gone. As late as 1810 there had been years when he was the only priest north of Halifax. "The want of clergy in these countries is distressing, deplorable and shameful in the extreme," he wailed. What help that was sent in the form of missionaries was often unreliable.[1] The only way to ensure a succession of priests, he believed, was to train young men from the community. For this he needed a seminary.

The obstacles to MacEachern's dream were twofold. Firstly, it required financial resources the parish didn't possess. And secondly, it was technically illegal, at least under the Colony's current laws. The solutions were simple — get the Pope to declare the Island a separate Diocese, and get the Legislature to change the law. As friends in Rome laid siege to the Vatican, MacEachern got to work in Charlottetown.

By 1830 everything had fallen into place. Rome had designated MacEachern the first Bishop of Charlottetown, a fully independent Diocese. And the Legislature, somewhat reluctantly, passed its own version of Britain's Emancipation Act, restoring to Catholics full rights of citizenship. In 1831 MacEachern opened his seminary at St. Andrews.

---

[1] MacEachern's difficulties with and attitude toward missionary priests from Ireland gained him a reputation for prejudice that may or may not have been justified. It was part of a quiet but intense struggle between the Scots and Irish congregations for control of the Diocese. Thanks in part to the head start MacEachern gave the Scots, the Island would wait until 1913 for its first Irish Bishop.

Bishop MacEachern died in 1835. His forty-five-year tenure on the Island was impressive. Founder of a Diocese and builder of eighteen churches. Enough foot miles logged to have circumnavigated the world. Twice. Creator of a seminary that became a college that would become a university. And leader of a Catholic population that had, by the time of his death, grown to fifteen thousand. "Father MacEachern is adored by his people." Although written at the start of his ministry, it could have been his epitaph.

Tom Douglas

The poor are left to Providence's care. They prowl like other animals along the shore and pick up limpets and other shellfish.... Hundreds thus annually drag through the season a wretched life, and numbers unknown, in all parts of the western Highlands, fall beneath the pressure, some of hunger, more of the putrid fever, the epidemic of the coasts, emigrating from unwholesome food, the dire effects of necessity.

—Thomas Pennant, describing the Isle of Skye, 1772

om Douglas was born in 1771, the seventh son of Dunbar Hamilton Douglas, Earl of Selkirk. The Earl owned a fair chunk of Scotland, making his a good family to be born into. If you can't be born rich, be born lucky.

Tom Douglas was born both.

As a young man he became known as something of an intellectual — which in itself was something of an oddity for a British aristocrat. With six brothers before him, he stood little chance of inheriting much of the family fortune. Instead he prepared for the inevitability of working for a living. He studied law at the University of Edinburgh, and afterward continued his education with travel. He toured the Highlands, and even went so far as to learn Gaelic. He worked on one of his father's farms, to learn what a landlord should know. He travelled to France, and studied the Revolution there firsthand.

All the while — through, it must be emphasized, no fault of his own — Tom's brothers were dying. Tuberculosis, yellow fever, unfortunate encounters with difficult horses — one by one they passed away. By 1797 only Tom was left. Two years later his father died and the estate was his. Tom Douglas, Baron of Daer and Shortcleuth, fifth Earl of Selkirk. He was twenty-eight years old.

A less serious soul might have taken this extraordinary stroke of fortune as a sign to party one's face off. The new Earl of Selkirk had a better use for his new position. He would save Great Britain from the spectre of revolution.

He believed he could see the seeds that had produced France's bloody revolution taking root in Scotland and Ireland. Too many people trying to eke an existence from exhausted farmland. Too many more being squeezed to their last copper by greedy landlords, or thrown off the land entirely to make way for more profitable enterprises like sheep farming. Overpopulation and hopelessness — the two would destroy the kingdom if not addressed.

Selkirk had a simple solution. Emigration. Great Britain should help its poor and dispossessed settle in the Colonies. There they could become useful, productive citizens — an asset rather than a threat to the future.

Selkirk's peers were not convinced. They had an even simpler solution to the problems he identified — let the poor and dispossessed fend for themselves. And if they got desperate enough to threaten revolution? Execute them. That had worked in Ireland, after the failed rebellion of 1798. No reason to think it wouldn't work again. In addition to this, there was great resistance to the concept of assisted emigration. The end of the eighteenth century saw the armies of European countries grow to unprecedented sizes. How could Britain hope to keep up if it allowed, nay, encouraged its cannon fodder to move across the Atlantic Ocean? Not surprisingly, Selkirk's ideas met with little enthusiasm when he presented them to the Colonial Office.

A lesser man would have been discouraged, but Selkirk possessed the ultimate restorative — money. If the Government wouldn't help, he'd prove the idea on his own. First a small-scale emigration — to work the bugs out — then a larger effort. Once the value of the idea was proven, it should take off on its own. All he needed was land, and some dispossessed to settle it with.

His first choice for settlers were the Irish. Desperately poor and backward, Ireland was widely regarded as the basket case of the British Isles. Selkirk was touched by its plight, especially in the aftermath of the failed 1798 rebellion. But there was an ugly streak in British culture that had it in for the Irish. Some questioned, only half-jokingly, whether they were fully human. Even stubborn Selkirk couldn't overcome this prejudice. Reluctantly he shifted his focus to another oppressed society — the Highlanders of Scotland.

The next problem was to find a suitable site in North America to settle them on. He mused over Louisiana, but it was French (soon to become American) territory. A more realistic choice was Upper Canada, and he began to negotiate for a large tract near Sault Ste. Marie. But the Government hinted it might be more co-operative if he chose a "maritime situation." Obligingly, he switched his plans to Prince Edward Island.

By the summer of 1803 everything was in place. His recruiters had signed up eight hundred prospects from various places in the Highlands. Protestant and Catholic, selected from a variety of Clans, it was one of

In July they set sail for Prince Edward Island.

the biggest mixed emigrations to ever leave Great Britain. In July they loaded onto three hired vessels —*Polly*, *Dykes* and *Oughton* — and set sail for Prince Edward Island. Selkirk was with them, eager to observe his experiment at work.

The first settlers landed at Orwell Bay in early August. A few days later, Selkirk himself came to see how they were doing. "I arrived at the place late in the evening," he recalled, "and it had a very striking appearance. Each family had kindled a large fire near their wigwam, and round these were assembled groups of figures, whose peculiar national dress added to the singularity of the surrounding scene. Confused heaps of baggage were everywhere piled together; and by a number of fires the whole woods were illuminated."

"There cannot be a more extreme contrast to any old cultivated country, or a scene more totally new to a native of these kingdoms, than the boundless forests of North America," he argued. "An emigrant set down in such a scene feels the helplessness almost of a child." Thus it was vital to support them in getting established. Despite the lateness of the season and squabbles among themselves, Selkirk's settlers quickly adjusted to their new situation. The relative ease with which they settled in was the ultimate argument for his radical ideas.

History would have been tidier — and Selkirk might have died happier — if he'd stopped here. Or continued to concentrate on Prince Edward Island. But the Island was intended to be but the beginning of a much grander design. He planned to repeat the feat, on a much larger scale, in the Red River Valley of Manitoba. Here he ran up against a force even bigger than him — the North West Company. The Company's specialty was the fur trade, and it considered settlers as very bad for business. It attacked the Red River Settlement — both physically and in the courts. Warring with them wore Selkirk out. His health began to fail and the family tuberculosis took root. He died in 1820, not quite fifty years old.

C. D. Smith

ver its first fifty years as a British colony, the Island had more than its share of colourful Governors. Walter Patterson, who stole from the rich, and kept it. Edmund Fanning, who left his previous post in Carolina one step ahead of a revolutionary lynch mob. Joseph Frederick Wallet DesBarres, surveyor and adventurer.[1] He generated some of the finest maps of his era and celebrated his hundredth birthday by dancing on the Vice-Regal tables in Halifax. But even amongst this impressive slate of rogues and rascals, Charles Douglass Smith stands out.

Smith was born in 1761, the son of a half-pay[2] army officer. Although Smith Sr. had resigned from the army in disgust, he didn't stop any of his three sons from choosing military careers. The youngest, John Spencer, became a successful diplomat after his army service. The eldest, William Sydney, was a vice-admiral in the Royal Navy who later became Admiral-in-Chief for the Sultan of Turkey. And Charles Douglass? Well, it was fortunate he had brothers in high places.

He spent most of his army career alternating between service as a junior officer and languishing on half-pay. He saw some action during the American Revolution, but didn't manage to distinguish himself very much. By 1798 he'd risen to the rank of Lieutenant Colonel, but without a title or very powerful patrons, he knew

---

[1] Or, as one historian has commented, with more accuracy than charity, the Island's first three governors were: "A rogue, a knave, and a fool — in that order."

[2] Half-pay was the British Army's reserve system. It was like a retainer. When there wasn't a war on, the Army took the officers it didn't need, gave them half of their regular pay, and told them to stay ready until required. Lest this sound like too sweet a deal, keep in mind that even full pay wasn't enough for most officers to survive on unless they had an independent income.

he'd gone as far as he could in the Army. By 1812, on half-pay for over a decade, he was drifting into an obscure retirement when his brother Sydney rescued him.

On Prince Edward Island, years of low-level bickering between Governor DesBarres and his Chief Justice, Caesar Colclough, had blossomed into almost-open warfare. The Colonial Office's solution was to sack the both of them. Now it needed "an Active and Efficient Officer" to serve as a new Governor. Admiral Smith had a quiet word with his friend the Colonial Secretary. A few weeks later his brother Charles was on his way to his new posting.

He arrived in the Colony in the summer of 1813. Although the acting governor assured him he would find the citizens to be "a peaceable, regular and well-satisfied people," Smith soon decided differently. There were suspicious numbers of "Despicable, degenerate members... of the Yankey Tribes... from regions of Rum and Rascality." There were also far too many Roman Catholics, living with much more freedom than the law allowed. Then there were the Highlanders, "whose want of Industry, Sobriety and Agricultural knowledge is so great it is really wonderful how they have ever advanced toward prosperity at all." Even worse, the Island was a known hotbed of political radicalism. What with the Americans again at war with Great Britain, he suspected the colony was merely waiting for the right moment to rise in rebellion. His predecessor had ruled with a slack hand.

Governor Smith wouldn't make the same mistake.

His worst fears were confirmed as soon as he called the House of Assembly to meet. They wouldn't listen to his orders, refused to pass vital legislation reforming the militia and were under the control of "a Confederacy of a very dangerous description known as 'The Club.'"[3] After two months he dismissed the Assembly and decided to run the Colony by decree.

Aside from the intractable Assembly, Smith was most concerned with the state of the Colony's defence. After all, the Americans could attack at any time. The garrison of regular troops was tiny, and Smith had no faith in their ability to defend the Colony. The "most undisciplined" militia he considered even more unreliable. Luckily they now

---

[3] They were also sometimes known as "The Loyal Electors." A loose collection of like-minded MHAs, the Loyal Electors were one of the first organized political parties in British North America. At the time, though, formal political parties were regarded in some quarters as a threat to British-style democracy.

Henry decided to hurry the proceedings....

had an experienced military officer to whip them into shape. Unfortunately, they weren't so willing to be whipped.

Questioning Smith's authority to revise their regulations, the militia grew increasingly unmanageable. Things came to a head in 1815, when a company in Charlottetown mustered, but refused to obey his orders. "Insubordination!" he cried, and ordered their captain to punish them. The captain refused and instead resigned his commission on the spot. "Mutiny!" Smith thundered, and ordered the Garrison's company of regular troops to surround the rebellious militiamen. This they did, but when Smith ordered them to open fire, the garrison commander balked. Refusing an order was one thing — murder quite another. The enraged Governor had him arrested and reported the incident to the Atlantic region commander, Sir John Sherbrooke.

Sherbrooke, soon to be Smith's own superior as Governor-in-Chief, suggested the Governor might have over-reacted. He ordered the garrison commander released from jail, and then had the garrison reduced to twenty-two men. Governor Smith, he explained, had a tendency to "interfere unnecessarily with the troops."

The betrayal convinced Smith he was surrounded by enemies. The Loyal Electors, allied with Irish republicans and possibly the Free Masons, were conspiring to destroy him. He moved into the Officers' Quarters at the Garrison and had a permanent guard of loyal militiamen mounted. The list of those he could trust dwindled as, one by one, he had fallings-out with virtually every officer in his Government. Once out of the Governor's good books, there was no getting back in. Soon, High Sheriff John Edward Carmichael (his son-in-law) and his own son Henry were the only ones he truly trusted.

In 1817 he recalled the House long enough to dissolve it, hoping that a general election would produce a more tractable body. Alas, the new Assembly was also dominated by "the Diabolical Club," and after one session he ordered it adjourned. In this he was ably assisted by his son Henry, who decided to hurry the proceedings by knocking out several windows. Since it was January, the Members soon noticed. When questioned by the Speaker what had happened to the windows, Henry conceded: "I up and smashed 'em with my fists!" He was arrested, but when the House was dissolved, it lost its power to press the charge. Nineteenth-century democracy in action.

Another set of elections in 1820 produced similar results. On dismissing this House, Smith noted "there is no necessity to call another General Assembly for Years." The amazing thing is how well the colony continued to function, despite this state of seeming anarchy. To the dismay of his opponents, Governor Smith.ran a very frugal administration. He extracted statute labour for most of his public works, and thus could get by with little in the way of revenue. He needed House approval to raise additional taxes, but found he could get by without them. If he didn't need money, the House of Assembly had very little influence over him.

Smith's downfall was not his paranoia. Or his competence. Or his autocratic manner. Governor Smith fetched up on the nemesis of all his predecessors — the Land Question. Gradually he began to raise the ire of the powerful landlords who lived in Britain. He threatened escheat if they didn't pay their back quit rents. He actually began proceedings on two sparsely settled estates. His mistake was obvious. He could run the Colony any way he wanted. Flaunt democracy. Threaten to shoot the colonists.

Just don't mess with the landowners.

As the Colonial Office began to receive complaints from offended landlords, Smith's opponents in the Colony renewed their assault. In a self-fulfilling prophecy, they met in secret, for they knew the Governor would have them arrested if they met openly. They assembled a huge petition demanding Smith's recall. When he caught wind of what was afoot, Smith indeed had the leaders arrested for sedition. But the petition was got safely away to London, and the Colonial Office slowly ground into motion. They refused to sack the unpopular Governor, but managed to persuade him to resign by offering an annual pension of £500. This he accepted, and in 1824 bid the ungrateful Isle adieu. His was the last laugh. The generous pension came off the top of the Colony's annual grant. He collected it until his death.

In 1855.

Sometimes, Them Times Was Hard Times

he sunsets were spectacular, that summer of 1815. It seemed like every evening the sky blazed with red, orange and fuchsia. In England, the painter Constable was inspired to some of his best work.

The sunsets were caused by an Indonesian volcano named Tamboura. In April 1815, Tamboura spent two days creating the biggest explosion of the last seventy-five thousand years. One hundred and fifty cubic kilometres[1] of dirt and rocks went ballistic. People heard the explosion eighteen hundred kilometres away. An impenetrable cloud of dust a thousand kilometres wide spread over the Pacific. Ashfall, gas, flying rocks and tsunami killed ten thousand people. Another eighty thousand died in the famine and cholera that followed. Even more sinister was the fine layer of dust that drifted into the atmosphere. Acting as a global sun block, it lowered average temperatures by 1.5 degrees Celsius. Pretty sunsets soon gave way to very chilly nights.

News of the eruption never made it to the Island. By 1815, Islanders were absorbed in their own woes.

It was a time of peace, for all the good that did. The short war with the Yankees was over, but the freeze it had inflicted on emigration was still in effect. The longer war with France was also finally over, but with peace came an end to a very lucrative timber boom. Slow population growth meant fewer people to shoulder the tax load. Less work in the lumber woods meant less money all around.

Some areas were reeling from a recent rodential population explosion. Two years in a row, armies of field

---

[1] To get a hundred and fifty cubic kilometres of dirt, you'd have to excavate all of Prince Edward Island down to a depth of twenty-five metres.

mice had burst from the woods like a biblical plague, swarming through fields and houses, terrorizing the populace. Their tiny furry bodies washed up on beaches like rafts of seaweed. Settlers swore that if they dug a pit at night it would be full by morning. Predators caught so many, they died from overeating. It was dubbed "The Year of the Mouse." The effect on the harvest was not good.

All in all, global natural disaster might have picked a better time to visit Prince Edward Island.

In all his eighty-odd years, Benjamin Chappell of New London couldn't remember a winter as cold as the one of 1815-16. "Very cold as to make us miserable," he wrote in his diary on January 27. "Saturday was much colder this year — very cold — very cold," he wrote in February. "The weather continues so cold that little business can be done — so many people frost burnt Mrs. Moore house is crowded with them." It might have been that Chappell was just feeling the cold more as he got older. But Island winters weren't new to him. He'd been through more than forty of them.[2] This one was different.

Bitter winter gave way to a cold, dry spring. "Some rain Bless God," Chappell noted on May 28, "so the grass is beginning to grow, but this is two weeks later than before — great death amongst the cattel."

At least, in this disaster, the Island wasn't alone. On June 6, a storm dumped several inches of snow on Quebec City. Carriages had to plough through axle-high drifts. "In almost every house the stoves are regularly heated the same as in winter," reported the press. Flurries kept up for two days. The same snowstorm swept through Nova Scotia, and probably sent a few flurries through Prince Edward Island. All across the continent, spring sowings were either dangerously late or under unexpected snowfall. "Precautions against scarcity cannot be too generally recommended," a Nova Scotian paper warned. "Nothing which may provide sustenance for men and beast ought to be neglected."

By the autumn the prospects were grim. Harvests had either failed completely, or were sharply down. The winter of 1816 had been cold. The winter of 1817 was going to be cold and hungry.

Desperate times call for desperate measures. The Island was fortunate in having just the desperado to deal with the situation — their spectacularly unpopular Governor, Charles Douglass Smith. Paranoid, despotic, bad-tempered and with the diplomatic skills of a wounded

---

[2] Including the winter of 1775, which so impressed young Thomas Curtis. Chappell actually put Curtis up for a few nights, and no doubt heard his lament to the Island climate in great detail.

bear, C. D. Smith was ideally suited to deal with this potential disaster.

"The season of scarcity which has lately affected so many countries has to a certain degree extended to the Island," he announced. For the most part, the Colony's harvest was better than those on the mainland. The main danger was in the marketplace. The Colony was a net exporter of foodstuffs. Shortages on the mainland would mean higher prices. And the temptation for some landlords and farmers to sell their harvest at a premium price — even if it meant their neighbours might starve. Governor Smith took steps to remove all temptation. At the start of the fall shipping season, he issued a decree. No vessel carrying wheat, barley, oats, flour, oatmeal, bread or potatoes would be allowed to leave Island ports.

It was drastic, but it worked.

Fate, and the Governor's stern measures, meant the bulk of the disaster passed over the Island. In Halifax, the poor saw bread — the staple of their diet — double in price in less than two months. Calls for relief funds soon began to mount. It's significant that the two counties that had the most trade with Prince Edward Island consumed over a third of the Nova Scotia relief budget. In Quebec, Governor-in-Chief Sherbrooke had to cajole and scold his Legislature into granting funds for the poor. Over £70,000 went to relief. This wasn't enough, and by February of 1817 Sherbrooke followed Smith in issuing a ban on food exports.

Though quick with the decree, Smith didn't prove so generous with relief funds for those unfortunate Islanders who needed it. After all, he might have reasoned, the Colony's entire budget was only £1,700 per year. Even if he'd been inclined to spend money on relief, there was little to spare. And he wasn't much inclined. He based his power on the fact he could run the Colony at a profit. He had no intention of squandering money on charity.

Citizens in other colonies got free bread to see them through the crisis. Islanders got the right to cut marsh hay on crown lands — for the price of the hay less the cost of cutting it. Other colonies spent thousands of pounds on relief funds. Smith allocated £100 in loans to buy seed grain and potatoes — to be repaid after the 1817 harvest.

Some Islanders arranged for their own relief. As the winter of 1816-17 wore on, Governor Smith reported that people were cutting firewood — illegally — at Fanningbank, the Lieutenant Governor's farm. He offered a £5 reward for the culprits. It was never collected. His son-in-law, High Sheriff John Carmichael, also charged that settlers "were set-

The dust of Mount Tamboura continued to filter down.

ting nets in rivers at unproper seasons in unproper manners." He warned there was a £5 fine for the offence. It was never levied.

In the sky, the dust of Mount Tamboura continued to filter down. The sun regained its strength, and the climate resumed its normal course. By the spring of 1817 it appeared that the measures taken — both legal and illegal — were going to see the Colony through the crisis. Almost timidly, the ban on food exports was lifted. Then, in a rare moment of good feeling between Governor Smith and his Legislature, they praised him for his handling of the crisis — "one of the soundest exercises of the power confided to you."

That May, Benjamin Chappell planted his potatoes just when he usually did, and they began to sprout. That July he recorded the arrival of fine, warm, summer weather. Just when summer usually arrives on Prince Edward Island.

Pearce and Abell

ome time towards the end of last century an old man was struggling through a church service in Fortune. He was tired, the sermon — dull. For these good reasons, he fell asleep. When he awoke with a start the Minister was preaching on how Cain killed Abel. "You're wrong sir," the old man interrupted. "It was Pat Pearce killed Abell, and I can show you the exact spot!"

In 1819 Edward Abell was the estate agent for the Hon. James Townshend's holdings on Lot 52, which centred around Fortune. Abell was not the most popular man in the settlement. An early visitor to the estate, Captain Frederick Marryat met him in 1811: "From what I could see of him, he appeared to be rascal enough for the stewardship of any nobleman's estate in England."

"I guess he was a good enough man for the people he was working for," recalled a neighbour many years later, "but he was a cruel son-of-a-gun." As bad as Edward Abell was, people remembered his wife Susannah as worse — "A veritable virago — a selfish and unscrupulous woman who goaded Abell on to acts of harshness and injustice." She once even had to answer charges of assault on one of her servants.

The courts were a familiar place for the Abells. They issued so many summonses and foreclosures on their tenants they wore out several justices of the peace. They may have been merely big fish in a small pond. (Or, at this stage in Island history, small fish in a big puddle.) But they were, in the stead of their employer, *de facto* rulers of Lot 52.

The hero of our story was Patrick Pearce — a retired soldier and, as we will see, a dab hand with a bayonet. Pearce came out in 1811, among seventeen families of Irish emigrants recruited by James Townshend to settle the Fortune estate. He took out a standard lease; one hundred acres of uncleared land at 1 shilling per acre. For the next eight years he lived a quiet life. Cleared his land. Built a cabin. Paid his rent on time. No trouble with or to anyone. Until Susannah Abell took a fancy to a fine black carriage horse Pat Pearce happened to own.

August was rent time for the Island's tenant farmers. As Edward Abell made his way to the Pearce place it was obvious he had another agenda. Susannah wanted that black horse, and her husband had every right to seize it if Pat Pearce could not raise his rent. On the face of it, this presented a problem. Pearce was a good tenant who had never missed his rent. He'd had no mishaps the previous year, so there was no reason he'd be forced to pay his rent in horse instead of cash. But Edward Abell had the law, and a dandy loophole on his side.

The lease Pearce had signed in 1811 called for his annual rent to be paid in sterling currency. Sterling was so rare on the Island there was even a proverb about it in the neighbouring colonies. "The sight of a coin," went the saying, "will bring a tear to an Islander's eye quicker than an onion." Okay. So it wasn't a classic, as proverbs go. But it was an accurate observation. Cash currency was scarce. Most land agents accepted rent in produce or in local currency at a set exchange rate. But what if a land agent wanted to put a tenant over a barrel? He could demand the exact terms of the lease, then watch his victim scramble.

Pearce had his rent ready. He gave Abell twenty shillings in local and sterling currency. When Abell refused to accept the local stuff, Pearce made frantic visits to his neighbours and managed to get his local tokens converted to acceptable coin. When he returned, he found the land agent had summoned a bailiff and was about to take the horse. As Abell took the money, he reminded Pearce the quit rent was also due. Quit rent was the money a landowner owed the Crown for granting him the land in the first place. Technically, quit rents were the responsibility of the landowner, not the tenant. But, since tenants had few rights or recourse, they were often saddled with this, as well as their regular rents.

Pearce made another frantic tour of his neighbours, and managed to convert or borrow enough coin to cover the extra demand. Once again he returned to his farm.

He found Edward Abell sitting on a stump, resting. The land agent, after all, had had a very trying morning. The bailiff was off getting a witness so that the seizure of the horse would be nice and legal. When Pearce thrust the quit rent money at him, Abell cooly refused to accept it. When the bailiff returned, he saw Pearce and Abell arguing hotly over the situation. He then saw Pearce break off shouting and disappear into his cabin. He emerged seconds later with a musket. The weapon wasn't loaded, but a wicked, three-sided bayonet was fixed to the barrel. Pat Pearce, you recall, had been a soldier.

He obviously remembered his bayonet drill. He stabbed Edward Abell twice — once in the arm and once in the abdomen. Then he threw down the weapon and fled into the woods. The bailiff carried Abell to his house. He lingered there for two days, then he died.

Pat Pearce, you recall, had been a soldier.

Pat Pearce became a hunted man. Authorities issued a £20 reward for his capture. This was a huge sum — enough to pay four years' rent on a typical holding. Not one of Pearce's neighbours was tempted by it. They obviously felt that what he had done, if not legal, was certainly just. Edward Abell was murdered in August. Pat Pearce's people hid him all winter. We hid him in our cellar, a family would recall later. No, no, another would respond. We had him in our attic. Come spring, the story goes, he was smuggled onto a vessel anchored at Annandale, made good his escape and was never heard of again. The story suggests the vessel's captain was Nicholas Falla, one of the Justices of the Peace the Abells had been so fond of using.

William Cooper

n the 1830s the most powerful politician in the colony was a retired sailor named William Cooper. In the genealogy of political parties, he was the great-grand-dad of our modern-day Liberals. He led the first popular political movement in the Colony, and, for a few years, seemed on the verge of reshaping Island society.

Born in 1786, he spent much of his youth in the Royal Navy, and was said to have served at the Battle of Trafalgar. After the Wars he emigrated to Prince Edward Island and took a farm near Fortune.

In 1820 there was an unusual job opening in the Fortune area.

After Edward Abell's encounter with Patrick Pearce's bayonet, Lord James Townshend found himself in need of a new estate agent. He hired William Cooper. A strange beginning, when you think of it, for one who would be remembered as the leading radical of his time.

Cooper was, by all accounts, very good at his job. He collected the rent, signed up new tenants and didn't get bayonetted. All in all, he must have seemed everything Townshend was looking for in an employee. But Cooper had broader ambitions, and decided to try his hand at shipbuilding. Around 1829 he launched a little brig named the *Hackmatack*. Unfortunately, the market was flat and the boat lost money. Some of the money belonged to Cooper. Much more, it was alleged, belonged to Lord Townshend. When Townshend heard that some of his income was being speculated on shipbuilding, he fired Cooper by return post.

Looking back, many of Townshend's fellow proprietors must have wished their colleague had been less hasty.

It was, after all, the God-given right of every land agent to steal from his employer. A wayward Cooper taking the occasional, um, "unauthorized advance on salary" wasn't really a problem. An angry, aggrieved Cooper becoming a powerful politician — *that* was a problem. A problem that would plague the Island's proprietors for decades.

Having viewed the land system from the inside, Cooper became interested in reforming it. This was a fortunate choice, because Reform was a growth industry in the early 1830s. Echoing the Mother Country, the Island had just passed an act that extended the vote to Roman Catholics. Since the Island's population was nearly fifty per cent Catholic, this doubled the electorate overnight. Since most of the Island's Catholics were poor tenant farmers, it was unlikely many of them would be voting for the ruling Tories. Not if they had an alternative. William Cooper had an alternative.

"Our Country's Freedom and Farmers' Rights," read his election banners. At the heart of his platform was one of the oldest political tricks in the colony. Every proprietor who received a grant in the Land Lottery of 1767 had agreed to return the property to the Crown if he failed to meet certain conditions. The legal term for this process was "escheat." Since none of the original land grantees had honoured their obligations, the whole Island, in theory, was escheatable. As a political weapon, it had been used several times by cabals of resident landlords trying to take land from non-resident landlords. Cooper promised to turn it into a tool for land reform.

"There cannot be a greater power given to one man over another than the right of a landlord over his poor tenants," he thundered from the hustings. "The more I consider it, the more plain it appears to me that nothing less than a general Escheat will do justice, or satisfy the inhabitants of this Island." Take the land from the rascals who refuse to honour their obligations and give it to the farmers who farm it. It seemed not only just, but kind of patriotic. The new electorate was convinced, and William Cooper was launched on a new career.

"The more the question is agitated, the more clear truth and justice will appear." Cooper agitated the question at every opportunity in the House. To pay rent, he told his followers, "is to foster oppression and reward crime." If the Colony's tenant farmers simply refused to pay rent, he reasoned, the whole rotten system would crumble. At least, that's how the theory went. Cooper himself was careful to keep the rent on his own farm fully paid. Principle was one thing — prison was another. He was unable — or unwilling — to lead his party from a jail cell.

To pay rent is to foster oppression and reward crime.

Despite this lapse, the Escheat movement gained momentum. Cooper himself gained the attention of the Colony's ruling elite. "An artful person," reported Governor Charles FitzRoy, "but very illiterate — possessed of much low cunning and perfectly unscrupulous." Probably true, but the people loved him. Re-elected in 1834, he came out of the 1838 election with a clear majority in the House. The Establishment was appalled.

The monkeys had taken over the zoo.

Cooper found that merely winning the election was not going to bring sweeping land reform. In this era, the Lieutenant Governor was the Colony's true chief executive. He answered only to his superiors at the Colonial Office in London. The local House of Assembly could pass laws until the cows came home. The Governor didn't have to sign them unless he wanted to. Cooper thus decided to go over the Governor's head, and appeal directly to London.

It's hard to imagine the icy coldness of the reception William Cooper must have got in London. Society regarded property and wealth with an almost mystical reverence. Cooper was asking for a law to take property from the wealthy and give it to a bunch of poor, unpedigreed farmers. A Satanist at a revival meeting would have had a better hearing. Not only did he not get his legislation, he didn't even get an appointment.

To make this a good story, William Cooper should have died heroically in a shipwreck on the way home. At least then there would have been some rollicking good ballads composed in his honour. Instead, the return voyage was uneventful, and William Cooper slowly faded away. With its main plank reduced to splinters, the Escheat Party collapsed and was wiped out in the 1842 election. Although his loyal constituents returned Cooper himself, he had little interest and spent very little time in the House. After sitting out a few elections he tried a comeback, but the politics of radical land reform had lost their appeal. "When he was in England, he could find no one who would talk to him," quipped one opponent. "Now he can find no one to listen to him." It could have been his epitaph.

The Minister

It was hard to be a saint in a cold climate; the drudgery of the body is so insistent. On the holy day the best people would not light a fire or draw water from the well. To cut wood was beyond question. There was the known case of the man who merely gathered sticks upon the Sabbath day, and the congregation stoned him with stones, and he died. To cut wood was the ultimate act of defiance. Besides, the neighbours would hear the sound of the axe.

— Sir Andrew Macphail, *The Master's Wife*, 1939

On a cold, blustery day in February 1867, a procession of three hundred and fifty sleighs wound its way toward a cemetery in Orwell. At the head of the two-mile-long line was a hearse bearing the body of Reverend Donald McDonald. The McDonaldites were paying their last respects to The Minister.

Born in Perthshire, Scotland, around 1782, Donald McDonald was the son of a poor crofter. Luckily for him, Scotland was one of the best places in Europe for a poor person to get an education. When he was twenty-five he decided to attend the university at St. Andrews. Supporting himself by working as a teacher and farm labourer, he worked toward a degree in Divinity. He graduated in 1816 and was ordained as a Presbyterian minister.

His first posting was as a travelling missionary in the Highlands. Since his family had originated in the Highlands — his father had fought for Prince Charles in 1745 — he was fluent in Gaelic. However, the posting was the beginning of a tormented time for Donald McDonald. He was restless. Legend suggests he began to drink heavily. He himself hinted in later years he may have strayed from official favour. At any rate, by 1824 it appears that he and the Highlands had had enough of each other. He decided to emigrate.

He settled first in Cape Breton. It has been suggested that frontier North America was not the best of destinations for a person with a drinking problem. Travellers from Europe were constantly amazed at the abundance of alcohol in the New World — and the capacity of the inhabitants for consuming it. Possibly because of this, Cape Breton was not the fresh start McDonald had hoped for. Taking a church on the Bras d'Or Lakes, he had soon thoroughly scandalized his parishioners. Not only did he drink far too much, but he did far too much drinking with Catholics! Two years later he was on the move again. This time to Prince Edward Island.

The Minister was an electrifying speaker.

McDonald bottomed out here. Within a year he'd given up on preaching and was spending most of his time wrestling with his restless soul. "We would watch him," Murdoch Lamont remembered, "sitting on a hillock, reading his Bible, acting as if the reading of it caused him trouble. Then, with a perplexed look, he would retire out of sight."

Then one day, an unseen voice boomed through his head. "THE TIME IS COME." He remembered at first being quite alarmed. Where he'd come from, if an unseen voice told you the time is come, it meant life — either yours or everybody's — was about to end. Then he calmed down. The time is come, he realized, to go forth and spread the Word. The Minister had finally received his calling.

Prince Edward Island in the early 1830s was a good place to start your own religious sect. The New World was very scary to newcomers. If you'd never even seen an axe before, and you were faced with the prospect of hacking a farm out of wilderness, you needed all the reassurance you could get. Religion was a familiar, safe haven for people continually assaulted by the new and unfamiliar. Between 1830 and 1850, North America was swept by many surges of Christian revivalism.

In many ways, McDonald's ministry was the same as many others across the continent. Technically, it was merely a fundamentalist branch of the Church of Scotland that placed even greater emphasis on Biblical text. More unusually, it also emphasized the experience of personal, overwhelming conversion, like McDonald himself had experienced. But parts of the "McDonaldite" creed were unique.

The first was language. McDonald's flock were, for the most part, Highlanders. Their language was Gaelic. We tend to think that the Gaelic-speaking people of the Highlands were primarily Catholic. "Bonnie Prince Charlie," for instance, was Catholic. So were most of the major Clan Chieftains. No doubt, before the Minister came along, most Islanders would have thought this true as well. After him it was hard to make that mistake.

McDonald told his people they were special. Scattered by exile, toughened by their hard scrabble lives, he told them they might be The People, being tested for the coming Millennium. It was an intoxicating prospect, made even more thrilling by the sight of Donald McDonald in his pulpit.

For the Minister was an electrifying speaker. He could take his congregation into his hand and make them dance. Literally. An important part of the McDonaldite experience was "taking the works." As the glory of the message overtook them, the People might dance with religious ecstasy. The ignorant — or maybe envious — dubbed them "Kickers" or "Jumpers." But, as L. M. Montgomery warned: "Outsiders are often affected — even the most sceptical — and frequently take 'the jerks' as bad as the sect themselves."

Kickers, Jumpers, Jerks — the McDonaldites didn't seem to care much what others called them. They had the strength of numbers. Within twenty years, over ten thousand Islanders considered themselves followers of the Minister. Next to the monolith of Catholicism, they were the biggest single sect on the Island.

The power of McDonald's ministry is evident in the fact it lived on after his death. Now called the "Free Church of Scotland," it survives to this day. In addition to religious tenets, the Free Church was vital to the transmission of Highland culture. Well into the twentieth century, McDonaldite churches were still conducting their services in Gaelic — generations after the language disappeared in secular society. All the more testament to the power of Donald McDonald's personality. For he never allowed anyone to make his picture while he lived, and he never thought it necessary to write a book outlining his religious philosophy. He just spoke the word. And the People listened.

> Donald MacDonald would stride up to the pulpit, throw off his coat, roll up his sleeves and tear open his collar. Poising the big pulpit Bible upright, he would strike a hand downward into the pages. Wherever the book would open he would find his text and blaze forth into a sermon that held his auditors spellbound for two hours.
>
> For forty years he strode up and down the Island in periodic sorties from his stronghold in Belfast. His was a religion of old-fashioned intensity, with the fires of hell lashing in the foreground to consume the sinner and to spur the righteous.... He held them in the hollow of his hand. The Island still talks of him.
>
> — William Dutton, *The American Magazine*, 1929

The Ledger Giant

ames Yeo Sr. was a classic frontier success story. He came here with nothing and died the richest man in the Colony. Given his stature in Island history, the tendency is to imagine James Yeo as a giant of a man. He was in fact, quite small. But he was harder than an axe head and his ambition was exceeded only by his ruthlessness.

Born in 1789, he was the son of a Cornish shoe-maker. With little education and apparently less inclination to follow his father's trade, he was making a living as a teamster when a series of personal disasters struck. The death of his horse was followed swiftly by the death of his wife, leaving him jobless, penniless and with three small children to provide for. He was literally on the verge of starvation, and legend suggests he was trying to drink himself to death when his big break came.

A merchant named Tommy Chanter hired him onto a shipbuilding crew he was sending over to Prince Edward Island. In recent years Chanter and his partner Thomas Burnard had been making a respectable profit out of this sort of venture. Each fall they hired a crew and sent them out to property he owned in western Prince Edward Island. Over the winter they would cut timber and over the summer they would build a small trading vessel — one to two hundred tons registered weight. Then in the autumn they would load the new vessel with more timber and sail it back to Britain, where Chanter would sell both. It was a risky sort of venture, but when the home market was hungry for vessels and timber, the profits were most gratifying.

Recently remarried, James and his new wife Damaris made the voyage to Prince County in 1819. Yeo discovered an affinity for shipbuilding, and was soon promoted to foreman. Though he had no formal education, he had an amazing memory and a voracious appetite for learning every aspect of his new trade. In many ways, the shipyards of 1820s Prince Edward Island were James Yeo's university. He was an excellent student, graduating with honours. In 1829 he built a vessel of his own, a schooner named *Mary Ann*, and set himself up as a merchant and lumber dealer. A few years later he bought the shipyard and was on his way to being the biggest shipbuilder in the colony. But how, you may ask, did a man who came here with no penny to his name gather enough money in ten years to buy a complete shipyard? The answer indicates that Yeo learned how to do more than drive treenails during his apprenticeship.

As absentee landowners, Chanter and Burnard had many debts owing to them on the Island. James Yeo very thoughtfully set out to collect them. He might not have known how to read very well, but he did know how to serve a writ. And perhaps more importantly, he had the energy to serve lots of them. "For six months he'd never go to bed," one man remembered. "He'd go into a tavern or halfway house and have a few drinks and get a lunch and lay down in a chair to sleep for a couple of hours. Then he'd go out in the saddle again. I seen him go past Cascumpeque, and he'd be sound asleep in the saddle with the horse just walking along — Yeah, he was quite a bird."

Soon the bird had collected enough money to build the *Mary Ann*. There was the possibility that the money he collected didn't actually *belong* to him. When Thomas Burnard died in 1825, Tom Chanter sold the Island end of the business to William Ellis, his master shipwright. Technically, the debts owing Burnard and Chanter also became the property of William Ellis. Some said that by collecting those debts and keeping the proceeds James Yeo *stole* that money. Others said that Yeo had been given the right to collect the debts in lieu of back wages. Yeo himself didn't seem to care much what anyone said. He had ensured that he and his family would never go hungry again. As long as people respected him, feared him and did what he wanted, they could say or think what they wanted.

By 1840 James Yeo had collected five more shipyards and was the most active shipbuilder on the Island. [Well, bully for him, you might snark. But remember. In these years only Great Britain itself built more vessels on a per capita basis than Prince Edward Island. Being *that* big in *that* industry in *this* place at *that* time was quite an achievement.] He owned the better part of twenty thousand acres. His wage bill was bigger than the colonial government's entire annual budget. He had become more than a mere shipbuilder. With wharves, yards, drydocks and warehouses in England and Prince Edward Island, he had become the

He'd be sound asleep in the saddle - the horse just walking along.

head of an international conglomerate. It was very much a family business. Damaris ran the store at Port Hill. His eldest son by his first marriage, William, managed the wharfs and yards at the English end of the business. Younger sons and in-laws were soon launching vessels of their own. As an added bonus, William was also an experienced mariner capable of taking a turn at the family's growing fleet of deep-sea trading vessels. Detractors noted Yeo's rude origins and spread rumours that William had learned his skills in the lucrative but illegal slave trade. But they did so quietly. Because, by 1850, a good portion of Prince Edward Island and Devonshire were linked to the Yeo family's fortunes.

One story illustrates the drive and ruthlessness that made James Yeo so wealthy. One day, some time in the 1840s, a distraught sea captain came into a Charlottetown tavern to settle his nerves. The timber cargo he had been expecting to load, he bemoaned to the tavern keeper, was not ready. The tavern keeper pointed to a scrofulous little man sitting in a stupour at a corner table. Looks are deceiving, the keeper suggested. If anyone can get you a shipload of timber in jig time, it's that man there. The captain went over, roused James Yeo, and put the deal to him. Yeo rose, then rode all night to Port Hill and raised the tenantry. They worked like dogs, cutting, hauling and making the cargo ready. Did they do this for love or loyalty? No. They did it because they owed James Yeo money. Two days later, when the captain sailed into Richmond Bay, the cargo was ready.

With his business firmly established, James Yeo turned his mind to politics. He'd been poor. He certainly knew how ruthless poor people could be. Thus, once he was wealthy, he became a committed Conservative. The best way to keep others from doing the sort of stuff he'd gotten away with was through firm government.

In an era of open balloting, it was easy for someone like James Yeo to get elected. He simply made it known that the electorate was as free to vote against him as they were to pay their debts in full the day after they did. The platform was irresistible. From 1839 to 1867 he only lost one election.

He was not called the Ledger Giant for nothing.

James Yeo died in 1868. Fitting, considering the mid-1860s were the peak years for the Island's shipbuilding history. He died at the height of the Golden Age that made him possible.

The Oldest Islander

Last evening, at the Mechanics' Institute, was presented a somewhat novel theory which supposes the earth to be many thousands of years older than has been previously supposed by Philosophers.

— Morning News, 1845

ome time during the well-digging season of 1845, a man named Donald McLeod was digging for water near French River. About twenty feet down, he unearthed a queer-looking rock. It had teeth in it. Fangs, really. Though he was just a common well-digger, McLeod realized it wasn't every day you found a rock with fangs in it, so he set it aside to take home.

McLeod's find soon came to the attention of Abraham Gesner. A Nova Scotian, Gesner had been commissioned to do a geological survey of the Colony. More than a mere geologist, Gesner was also an avid amateur palaeontologist. His final report was bad news to anyone who hoped to make a fortune from mining on the Island. Under the dirt, he concluded, was more dirt. Some good for making bricks. Some good for making glass. However, he observed, you do have this really neat rock with fangs in it.

Some time around 1852, McLeod gave the toothed rock to William Dawson, a local geologist and, like Gesner, an avid palaeontologist. Though Dawson was largely self-taught, he had impressive academic connections. One of his friends was Sir Charles Lyell, the acknowledged founder of modern geology. Dawson told Lyell about the rock McLeod had given him. Lyell suggested he pass it on to Joseph Leidy, the top palaeontologist in North America, at the Philadelphia Academy of Natural Sciences.

No one realized it, Donald McLeod had made paleontological history.

The teeth were a dead give-away. When the rock arrived in Philadelphia, Leidy examined it and concluded it was part of a face. Probably one of those newfangled dinosaurs people had been digging up lately. He named it Bathygnathus Borealis, *Leidy* — a ten-dollar title meaning "jaw-found-in-a-well-up-north, named-by-Leidy." Since bird-like dinosaurs were then being discovered in Nova Scotia, he suggested the fossil might belong to the same group. Then he had it numbered, catalogued and put so deep into storage that no one thought about it for another century. Professionals call this "museumizing."

In 1963, someone had another look at the Bathygnathus fossil. It wasn't a dinosaur at all, they realized. It was a dimetrodon. Probably the first to ever be discovered. Though no one realized it, Donald McLeod had made paleontological history.

Imagine a wind-surfing board with legs. And a head. That's sort of what a complete Bathygnathus would have looked like. Often called a "sail-back dinosaur," it's actually much older than the dinosaurs. How much older? Well, if the dinosaurs had had palaeontologists — don't scoff, a lot can happen over 150 million years — they would have considered Bathygnathus mind-bogglingly ancient. Indeed, on the geological time scale, a Tyrannosaurus Rex is much closer to us than it was to the dimetrodons. In many ways, we are both descendants of Bathygnathus.

Donald McLeod probably wouldn't have believed you, if you'd described the world his rock with teeth had grown up in. Three hundred million years ago, when Bathygnathus fell into what would become a well in French River, Prince Edward Island was at the heart of a single super-continent. Walk ten miles north, and you were in Spain. Since we were then only a few hundred miles north of the equator, the summer was literally endless. Unfortunately, the nearest beach was five thousand miles away.

Even more remarkable is the fact Donald McLeod thought to save the fossil in the first place. The world he grew up in was just beginning to imagine the concept that the earth might be more than a few thousand years old. Theories suggesting this were considered exotic novelties. The science of geology was barely fifty years old. Its offspring, palaeontology, had been around for less than twenty years. In 1845, Charles Darwin was still trying to make sense of his field notes. Given the world view of his time, the very last thing Donald McLeod would have conceived is that the queer-looking rock he dug up was once part of an animal 300 million years old. I suspect we're lucky the rock had teeth.

Otherwise, if I'd been Donald McLeod, I'd have thrown it out with the rest of the debris.

But even if dimetrodons, being less glamourous, are not as popular as dinosaurs nowadays. Even if they were once very common animals, and their fossils are not that rare. And even if Donald McLeod didn't know what he found, when he found it — find it he did. The first dimetrodon fossil on record.

Mr. Gesner's Lamp

braham Gesner was a Nova Scotian. Born near Cornwallis in 1797, he was trained as a physician and surgeon, but soon gained a reputation in the infant field of geology. This is the capacity that brought him to Prince Edward Island in 1846.

The Government wanted to see what sort of mineral wealth the colony might possess. Not that there was anything wrong with agriculture and shipbuilding — the dual backbones of the economy. It's just that it would be nice to know if there was anything more, ah, profitable under the farmland. It hired Gesner, one of the leading geologists in the Colonies, to come and do a geological survey.

He arrived in the summer of 1846. As a bonus to his survey work, he agreed to give a series of talks at the local Mechanics' Institute. This was a combination social club and self-improvement society devoted to giving elevating lectures to common people. Those expecting a discourse on geology were disappointed. Geology, you see, was only Gesner's day job. In his spare time he was something of an inventor. Even so, there was so much interest in the programme that it had to be moved to the court-house on Queen Square. The topic for June 19 was entitled "On Caloric Heat." Mr. Gesner intended to demonstrate a new type of lighting fuel he'd been working on.

Abundant artificial light was a luxury in this era. Houses could be lit with betty lamps, candles or whale oil, depending on the family budget. Whale oil gave the best light, but was prohibitively expensive — the process of hunting, killing and melting whales being quite an involved one. You'd not be in the habit of lighting the whale oil lamp every evening unless an abundant income

Abraham Gesner changed this.

flowed through your pockets. Most resorted to whale oil only on special occasions. The common illuminator was candlelight. Dim, flickering and themselves none too cheap, candles symbolized a world where the rhythm of daily activity was firmly fixed to the sun.

He'd devised a process to distill a flammable fluid from ordinary coal. When put in a lamp it was as clear as water, and burned with a clean, bright flame that rivalled that of whale oil. Because of the waxy residue left by the distillation process, Gesner dubbed it "wax-oil" or, in sort of classical Greek: "kerosene." It would soon be in commercial production, selling for a twentieth the price of whale oil. As it took over the marketplace, clean, abundant artificial light became commonplace. Kerosene freed household lighting from the necessity of deep pockets.

And the first time it ever burned in public was on that late spring evening in the old court-house on Queens Square.

No one at the time realized they were witnessing the beginning of a social revolution. Or the public birth of the modern petrochemical industry. Gesner himself still considered the research a work in progress — he hadn't even come up with the name of the stuff yet. He got to work on the geological survey, which he completed by the end of the summer. Elegantly written, it regretfully reported the Island was hiding nothing in the way of mineable metals or minerals. His job here done, he returned to Nova Scotia. After a few interruptions, he resumed work on his lamp fuel. In 1852 he gave it its name. In 1854 he patented the process. It was only in later years he recalled how the Charlottetown lecture had been kerosene's first public demonstration.

Good thing somebody remembered.

Belfast

What do you get when you mix four hundred Scotsmen and Irishmen together?

On the first of March, 1847, you got several hundred dented heads, a pile of broken cudgels and, by the best estimate, three dead. It started off as the Belfast by-election. It's remembered as the Belfast Riot.

As you may have been gathering, Islanders in colonial times found many things to hate about each other. Some were good, honest, Old-Country animosities, like Protestant and Catholic, Irishman and Scot. Others were modern tensions based on politics and income. Tories and Reformers — Snarlers and Snatchers, as they called each other — each feared utter catastrophe if the other got in and/or stayed in power. Those who farmed their own land feared and mistrusted the tenant farmers who could only afford to rent.

In many areas, these communities were buffered from each other by forest or lightly settled land. Around Belfast, one of the first parts of the colony to be heavily settled, the two were neighbours. The Scots had come to the area first, and so had the better and more prosperous farms. Many were even freeholders — owners of their own farms. The Irish, on the other hand, tended to live in the poorer "back settlements." In the regular routine of things, the two communities rarely rubbed shoulders. Except on election day. Then the possibility of sparks was always present.

Democracy has grown more sedate since the 1840s. Then there was none of this furtive skulking behind a curtain to scratch your ballot like some criminal. In the 1840s you congregated at a large platform called a "husting" on polling day. After listening to the candidates proclaim themselves and berate their opponents, you stood up proudly and shouted your choice for all to hear. If, of course, you were a male and had met the minimum property requirements. Another feature of the system was the length of time it took to complete the polling. Settlements were widely scattered, travel was slow and there were never enough electoral officers to go around. Polling thus took several days to complete.

The system demanded special strategies and tactics for success. The guiding principle was "strength in numbers." A party's supporters tended to vote in blocs, both to emphasize the popularity of their candidate, and to keep from being chased away by the other party's supporters. In a close election, a lone voter was not likely to vote at all.

The election of 1846 was close and hotly contested. The Colony's liberals, formerly known as "Escheators," now campaigned as "Reformers." The Colony's right wing, and currently its Government, was owned by the Tories. The Tories thought the escheat/reform movement had been safely crushed, and were annoyed at its resurgence. In addition, both sides were aware that the general drift in the Mother Country was toward giving colonial legislatures more power. The winner in 1846 would be well-placed to share out the slop from what promised to be a bigger trough.

In the Belfast area the electorate divided up fairly neatly. Irish Catholic tenant farmers tended to vote the Reform ticket, led locally by John Little, an Irish-born lawyer. The Tory ticket featured William Douse, a Scottish emigrant who had prospered as land agent for Lord Selkirk. He knew he could count on the district's Scots Presbyterian freehold farmers.

The election was held over two days in August, and although the Tories won a narrow majority of seats, they lost in Belfast. But Douse charged that an unusual number of his supporters had been chased from the polls before they were able to vote. He demanded the result be overturned and a new election held. Not surprisingly, the Legislature agreed, and ordered a by-election for the Belfast district. The polling was to begin on March 1, 1847.

The Tories had learned from the August result, and turned up at the hustings early and in numbers to vote. But many wandered off after casting their ballots. The Reformers arrived late, but they'd taken the precaution of inviting a number of interested observers from the Montague area. Though the latter had no right to vote in the district, they came to lend moral support. A little past noon they noticed they had gained an advantage in numbers. So, as a warm-up to their own voting, they decided to chase the remaining Tories from the hustings.

Crying for William Douse's blood, they tucked in with fist, foot and axe-handle. Douse saved himself by diving behind his supporters, and the Scots tried to stage a fighting retreat. Badly outnumbered, they were soon running for their lives.

They tucked in with fist, foot and axe-handle.

"I ran to the road," Alexander MacDougall remembered, "and on getting there I was struck from behind. I placed my hands over my head, thinking I would be murdered. They continued beating me. Some said: 'He has had enough.' Others said: 'He is dead.' And some said: 'Strike away.'"

After the one-sided battle, content they had secured the hustings, the Reformers began to vote. They did so, happily and quietly, for the better part of an hour. Then they noticed a rumble in the distance. The defeated Scots were returning to the field. They had reinforcements — two hundred or so — from Flat River and Pinette. With no thought of retreat, the Irish prepared to receive them. The Sheriff and his seven constables had no choice but to get out of the way as the two mobs came together.

"The field was as if a number of butchers had been at work," one participant remembered. Another recalled the unique sound of so many cudgels meeting so many heads. A hollow, sort of echoing noise, "like the simultaneous driving of wedges when a vessel was about to be launched."

This time it was the Irish who flinched first. They fled the field, closely pursued by the victorious Scots. Within minutes the only ones left at the hustings were the dead, the wounded and a handful of shocked election officials. The official death toll was three, but some maintained that the mobs had carried many more dead with them when they left the field. None of the three fatalities — a Scot and two Irishmen — were even registered to vote in the Belfast district.

As both sides nursed their bruises and buried their dead, the election was suspended. There was talk of moving the voting to Charlottetown, but the capital had no desire to host the event. The vote was finally held, back in Belfast, three weeks later. The Charlottetown garrison, a company of militia and a troop of cavalry stood guard over the hustings. There were no incidents. Possibly because there were also no Reform candidates. Fearing another violent clash, they withdrew before the final voting. The Tories won the election unopposed.

Colonel Sleigh

e came. He saw. He made rude comments.

His name was Colonel Sleigh.

Burroughs Willocks Arthur Sleigh was born in Lower Canada in 1821. Entering the British Army in 1844, he served for five years as a Lieutenant in the 2nd West India Regiment. After leaving the Army he embarked on a somewhat tumultuous business career. In 1849 he founded the Halifax and Quebec Railway. It failed. In 1850 he formed a mercantile company in England. It failed. The same year he founded a newspaper in Halifax — bankrupt within six months. Despite this dismal record, he announced in 1851 that he had bought the huge Worrell estate on Prince Edward Island. Five complete lots, over one hundred thousand acres. The selling price was £17,000.

In the spring of 1852 he swept into the colony, trailing promises and humbug like some cross between a carnival shill and a whirlwind. At a banquet organized to honour his arrival he seemed to divine the secret dreams of the Colony's business class. He announced his steamer, *SS Albatross*, would add Charlottetown to its New York-Halifax-Quebec route. He announced plans to found a bank, something the Colony had been dreaming of for a decade. He pledged to be kind, gentle and generous to his tenants. Even though he'd only been here a week, he had much sage advice to give respecting the land question, the fisheries and international relations.

Here, obviously, was a man who would get things done. Bemused but excited Islanders responded in kind. Sleigh was feted and celebrated. "See the Conquering Hero Comes," played the band as the House of Assembly put on a banquet for him. "The highest compliment ever paid an individual Islander," commented the Governor. He was named a Justice of the Peace. He was made colonel of the Castle Tioram Regiment — one of the Colony's most venerated Highland militias. And he wasn't even Scottish.

The bubble burst as quickly as it was spun.

By late summer, after two calls at Charlottetown, the *Albatross* had fled for more profitable waters. The Bank of Charlottetown came to naught. Some of his fellow aristocrats — men who had to scratch and fight for their positions in society — wondered why Mr. (ahem, Colonel) Sleigh was being elevated so quickly. They began to suspect he was nothing more than an elaborate Reform government plot to ridicule them.

Then some representatives of Mr. Worrell, former owner of the Sleigh estate, came to call. Evidently Colonel Sleigh had only put a down payment on his hundred thousand acres. A very small down payment. Mr. Worrell was extending a polite inquiry. "Where," he asked, "is the balance of my £17,000?" Suddenly, it was very hard to get an appointment with Colonel Sleigh.

They caught up to him in Halifax. He was stored in the city jail while they confirmed he was broke. After his release he sailed for England. Some members of the better classes began to wonder just who had been behind the banquets in his honour. Others denied they'd even been there. Needless to say, his colonel's commission was revoked.

Although Colonel Sleigh — he kept the title as a souvenir — never returned to the Island, he was by no means done with the place. In England he wrote a book: *Pine Forests and Hackmatack Clearings*. It was a sort of memoir of his experiences and adventures in the New World. Told, of course, from his point of view. It was a best seller. Lucky Prince Edward Island rated three full chapters. Call it Colonel Sleigh's revenge.

"The fame of Island lawlessness has extended to neighbouring provinces," he wrote. "When one hears you are bound for Prince Edward's, you perceive an involuntary shudder, and are favoured with a commiserating caution, such as a traveller from Italy would receive on announcing his attention to enter some well-known banditti pass."

It wasn't really the fault of Islanders, he conceded. They couldn't help how they'd been brought up, for "poverty, and its accompaniment, vice, nurtured by ignorance and petty cunning, did not form a favourable school whence the young Islander could draw wholesome experience from his sire." Islanders also couldn't help the poor example set for them by their social superiors. "Decayed tradesmen, pettifogging law-yers and ex-stockbrokers from the Mother Country tended not a little to inoculate the masses with that want of principle which unfortunately has taken root in the community."

"Where," he asked, "is the balance of my £17,000?"

The Colonel's main warning was the essential lunacy of giving the Colony responsible government — or, as he put it, "letting power pass into the hands of the lower orders." "It will hardly be believed in England," he wrote, "that the Premier keeps a grog shop. Any thirsty traveller can enter and purchase from the Honourable gentleman a noggin of gin. Your eyes will also be gratified, if of a republican turn, by seeing the ageing father of so exalted a son, wheeling an empty cask from the premises. Another personage in the Government is an ex-cook from a shipbuilder's yard. The remainder can be seen any day, selling farthing dips over the counters of their shops or driving their own waggons."

But what seemed to amaze and enrage Sleigh the most was the arrogance of the place that so quickly turned on him during his, ah, slight financial embarrassment. "Removed as they are from all intercourse with the world, these narrow-minded Provincials really fancy themselves par excellence THE people of British North America. "They require a lesson," you could almost hear him muttering in conclusion. "A couple of regiments would soon bring the Islanders to a sense of their own importance," he actually wrote.

Pine Forests and Hackmatack Clearings appears to have been the only success of Colonel Sleigh's life. After the splash of its publication, he settled in England. Tried his hand again at the newspaper business. No luck. Ran three times for the House of Commons. Defeated on each occasion. Started another mercantile business. Experienced another bankruptcy. When last heard from, he was musing how he might build a railway from Russia to India. He died in obscurity in 1869.

The Duellists

lexander Bannerman must have wondered just what the lunatics in London had been thinking. The new Lieutenant Governor had been appointed in 1850 to bring Responsible Government to the colony of Prince Edward Island. The mission was so important he had to brave the ice of the Northumberland Strait in a flimsy, open and very cold iceboat to get to his new posting. He arrived, safely, and he succeeded in implementing the new system. Islanders would now direct their own affairs — or at least most of them — through elected officials with real power. Then Bannerman discovered his new Colony seemed to have a flair for frontier justice you were only supposed to encounter in the lawless United States.

Eighteen fifty-one, you see, was a very good year for gunfights.

That summer saw the two most notable gun battles in Island history. In July, the land question reached new levels of discourse when landlord Donald McDonald was shot at his own gateway by unknown assailants. Of more serious tenor was the gunfire that occurred a month before in Charlottetown. On a fine summer evening, while the Governor was away, the capital was treated to the sight of the Premier of the colony facing the Leader of Her Majesty's Loyal Opposition. Over levelled pistol barrels.

On the grounds of the Vice-regal residence.

The Premier was George Coles. A successful brewer, distiller, merchant and farm-owner, he got into politics in the early 1830s. He first entered the Legislature as a Tory, but gradually drifted onto the side of the land-reformers. After the collapse of the Escheators in the early 1840s, George Coles picked up the pieces and rebuilt the Colony's left-wing party under the banner of Reform. He won the first election under the responsible government system, and thus became the Island's first real Premier.

"Jarge" Coles was a colourful politician, held in high regard by his electorate. His detractors sneered at his "low" origins. "It will hardly be believed in England," they scoffed, "that the Highest member of the Executive Council keeps a grog shop." Or sometimes dropped his grammar and said: "Me and the Governor." But George Coles' government was the first in seventy-five years to make progress toward solving the "Land Question," and its support of education made the Colony a world leader in school development.

The opposition Tories were led by Edward Palmer. They were probably feeling quite disgruntled in 1851. For the better part of a decade, since the defeat of William Cooper's Escheators, the Tories had things pretty much their way in the Island's Legislature. Then the Mother Country up and changed the rules, and suddenly their sworn enemies were in charge of the whole Colony. "A complete change of government," they moaned, "all the old officers turned out for a parcel of rascals!"

Palmer didn't seem to possess the personality to take setbacks in good humour. He, like Coles, had started his political career as a Tory in 1831. Unlike Coles, he stayed with the party. He also had a nickname, though not a very affectionate one. "Neddy Longlegs" was a comment on his gangly stature and exceedingly grave demeanour. "We have never seen him in happy, rollicking or joyous spirits," remembered one colleague.

The Governor had to fight hard to force the ruling Tories to give up their power and submit to popular elections. Afterward he remarked to his superiors: "How each party is ready to cut each other's throats ... I could have scarcely believed that such bitter animosity could have existed." But not even Bannerman would have dreamed where that animosity might lead.

The cause of the duel was never explained. It may have stemmed from something as simple as a difference over procedure. In the middle of June, Governor Bannerman left town on a visit to Kings County. In the absence of the governor, Colonial custom usually required the most senior military officer step in as acting Vice-regal. On the Island, though, the senior military officer was usually a very junior lieutenant. The custom that evolved here had the senior member of the Executive Council fill in for the Governor. Before Responsible Government, the Gover-

Palmer chose to stand to the east.

nor appointed whomever he wanted to lead his Executive Council. After Responsible Government, the elected premier automatically headed the governor's highest council.

Edward Palmer's keen legal mind immediately saw the problem. If the Premier was also the acting Governor, then he could sign his own government's legislation. Total anarchy, or worse — republicanism, could result! This was apparently the gist of the argument that wafted over the floor of the Assembly chamber on that June day. The exact tone used can't be replicated, but it certainly must have been sharp, because, after the set-to in the House, more words were exchanged on the Square outside. Palmer was deeply insulted, and sent a servant round to Coles' house later that evening to demand a retraction — or satisfaction.

Coles took this as a joke. It was bad enough to be sent a challenge by a servant, but when the servant wasn't even wearing a jacket? He sent the man away without an answer. Palmer then called Coles a coward. "Jarge" Coles had been called many things in his career, especially by his "social betters." This was too much. He responded with a challenge of his own. Palmer would make a public retraction, or there would be a "meeting." Palmer chose the latter.

The site selected was on Government House Farm — close to Fanningbank, the Governor's official residence. Probably near the kiddie pool of modern-day Victoria Park. The time was set for the evening of the twenty-first. Since it was no longer clear who had challenged whom, the seconds[1] had to flip a coin to see whose second would give the command to fire. The loser of the coin-toss got to choose where to stand. Coles won the toss. Palmer chose to stand to the east. With the niceties settled, the Premier of the Colony and his Opposition Leader paced off a distance, turned and waited for the command to shoot each other.

Edward Palmer fired first.

Though Coles was perfectly backlit by the setting sun, Palmer missed. As the echo of the shot died down, George Coles raised his own pistol. With great deliberation. And kept raising it until it was pointing straight in the air. Then he fired. Jarge Coles might not have been born a gentleman, but he knew how to behave like one.

---

[1] There certainly was a star-studded cast in attendance that evening. Palmer's second was Heath Haviland, a future Father of Confederation.

The Wreck of the Fairy Queen

 ny boat named the *Fairy Queen* must have been special, right? The very name conjures visions of a golden hull gliding gently through sunbeams — wafted on gossamer sails as the pixies flutter by.

Our *Fairy Queen* was a clapped-out dust bucket. A clumsy, underpowered paddle-wheeler — badly maintained and indifferently officered. She was leaky and had a bad habit of running into sandbars. Her crew was often rounded out at the last minute by whoever was hanging around the wharf willing to work for low wages. But her owners also owned the government mail contract. This meant she had the regular route between Charlottetown and Pictou, Nova Scotia.

If it was the early 1850s, and you were on a schedule and had to get to the mainland, the *Fairy Queen* was about the only game in town.

Friday, October 7, 1853, was a blustery day. Her Captain decided to delay sailing until noon, hoping the wind would die down. He was a young man, inexperienced in the ways of the sea and his new command. The wind continued to blow and several of the crew took the opportunity to nip ashore for a few last-minute drinks. Early in the afternoon the *Fairy Queen* sailed anyway, and was making a good passage. By suppertime she was nearing land at Caribou, just a few miles short of Pictou.

When the steering rope broke, no one was much alarmed. This was a common breakdown for the vessel, and the crew had lots of practice splicing it back together. But this was one break too many, and the repaired rope was too short to reconnect the wheel to the rudder. It was dusk by the time a new rope had been rummaged out of the hold and installed.

Meanwhile, the crew in the boiler room got bored and went up to see if they could help with the repairs. The fires died and the boilers went cold. *Fairy Queen* now had steering, but no power.

If it had been a calm evening, the scene might have been almost comical. Frustratingly close to land, rendered helpless by the parsimony of the owners (who should have installed steering chains, not ropes) and the incompetence of her crew. But the wind was gathering strength, and the steamer was wallowing helplessly in a rising sea. *Fairy Queen* was used to leaking, and relied on a steam pump connected to the main engines to keep her dry. With this pump down, and with waves breaking over the hatches, the boat was in danger of foundering. Soon the water broke into the engine room, making it impossible to rekindle the boilers. Powerless and listing, the steamer was only a mile from shore.

Fairy Queen was equipped with two lifeboats. The larger boat could take twenty-four people. The smaller could take ten. Since the vessel was only carrying twenty-six souls — thirteen passengers and thirteen crew — lifeboats should not have been a problem. The problem was in the oars. There were only four of them. The owners had ordered the rest put aboard a sister ship that had a longer run and, presumably, more use for them. Still, the Captain thought it prudent to launch the larger boat — both as a precaution and to get its weight off the sinking ship.

This is where things began to go very wrong.

As the large lifeboat was launched, several crew, including the Second Mate, decided it would be best if they went along to keep an eye on it. They weren't ordered to. They just piled in and drifted off to a safe distance to watch the steamer continue to settle. An hour later the Captain decided the *Fairy Queen* was past saving, and decided to try and abandon ship.

This was the plan: two crew, the women passengers and the cabin boy (the only child on board) would launch the small lifeboat. The crew in the large lifeboat, which was tied to the stern rail, would pull themselves back to the steamer, where the remaining passengers and crew would jump in. The two boats would then be lashed together and drift safely to shore.

This was the problem: as soon as the small lifeboat was swung out, the rest of the crew jumped in and cut it clear. They didn't wait for the women passengers. Or the cabin boy.

Time for an alternate plan. The Captain decided he might be able to persuade the crew in the large lifeboat to do their duty if he was there

At this point the Second Mate had enough of duty and took charge.

to encourage them. He tied himself to a rope and swam over. Against their better judgement (and sense of self-preservation), he got his Mate and crew to haul their boat back to the stricken steamer. They were within a few feet of the stern when a wave threw their boat against the *Fairy Queen's* hull. At this point the Second Mate had enough of duty and took charge. "I would not have gone alongside again for £500," he recalled when safely ashore. "Not for all of Pictou. My life is worth as much to me as any other person's!" He advised the Captain to go to the back of the boat. The Captain protested, but a crewman, who happened to be wielding a large oar, also suggested it might be best if he retired to the stern of the lifeboat. They then reeled their boat out to a safe distance. Moments later, the rope tying them to the steamer mysteriously parted and the *Fairy Queen* was on her own.

Twelve passengers and two crew watched the lifeboats drift away. A survivor, Mr. Lydiard, recalled shouting after them: "You are leaving us. I cannot curse you — I hope you live to repent your guilt, but if God in his providence should preserve my life, which I feel he will, I will meet you again!" [I envy Mr. Lydiard's restraint, whenever I read this passage. I know that if I'd been in his shoes, I would have been cursing the @#$%*&! swine with everything in my repertoire.] On board the lifeboat, the Captain ordered his heroic crew to make for shore as fast as they could, hoping he might be able to arrange a rescue boat before the *Fairy Queen* sank.

Once more, his plans came to naught. At midnight the castaways gathered on the *Fairy Queen's* upper deck, the only part of the boat still above water. As she continued to settle, the waves began to smash the deck cabins. Then, as she gave a lurch and broke in two, all were thrown into the water. The stronger were able to hold onto wreckage and float ashore. The rest were swept away.

The next morning a rescue tug from Pictou came across the scene. *Fairy Queen's* bow was still floating at anchor. Her stern was bobbing peacefully a little distance away. There was no trace of survivors. Seven people, including all five women and the cabin boy, were dead.

There are a number of postscripts to the sinking of the *Fairy Queen*.

PS #1: The boat's owners, Captain and crew were widely vilified when the story of that night came out. But the inquiry into her sinking became more a political event than a quest for justice.

PS #2: Only ten days after the wreck of the *Fairy Queen*, a sister ship, the *Commodore*, sank in the Bay of Fundy.

PS #3: Folk in Charlottetown for years after swore that at midnight on October 7, 1853, at the exact moment the *Fairy Queen* gave in to the angry sea, seven ghostly lights were seen to enter the Kirk of St. James. One for each victim of the wreck.

Damn Clever,
These Islanders

he mid-1800s was the Golden Age of Science on Prince Edward Island. For such a small place, fairly out of the way and with no industrial tradition, the Island has a surprising number of scientific firsts in its history. The first dimetrodon fossil ever discovered. The first kerosene lamp ever lit. The first underwater telegraph cable in the Western Hemisphere. The first horseless carriage in Canada. The grand-daddy of the modern ball-bearing and the world s first egg carton. To say nothing of more patented potato diggers that you can shake a hoe at. All had their debut on Prince Edward Island.

Where would the Age of Technology have been without us? For instance, folklore suggests, though history can't prove, that the Stillson wrench was actually invented by a Uigg blacksmith named McClosky, who sold the tool's prototype to American Daniel Stillson in 1869. For, of course, a pittance. Even in our folklore, we can't seem to get the best of a Yankee.

Then there was Laurette Doucette of Kildare Station. In 1889 he claimed to have invented a flying machine. Although there's no evidence he ever actually got off the ground with it, his neighbours did pay a dime just to see it. And honoured Laurette with the nickname L Oiseau.

Through the 1860s and '70s, the patent office saw a veritable stampede of bona fide Island inventors. Five improved potato diggers, a lath maker, a hay carrier, a Reversible Extension Carriage, a Treble Purchase Tree Stumper, and even a machine gun.[1] For various reasons,

---

[1] Invented by Tom Heustis of Seacow Head — a made man, if ever there was one, predicted the local newspaper. Although he wasn't made in any way by his idea, you must

He also demonstrated that he was more than a one-invention wonder.

P. John Burden

none of the above left much of a mark on world history. You can't say the same, though, about Watson Duchemin.

Duchemin was born near the outskirts of Charlottetown. His main trade was pump and block making. Pumps and blocks were two essentials of the wooden shipbuilding industry. Even the best-built vessels experienced seepage through their hulls, and thus required reliable hand pumps. And no vessel could manage its sails without blocks.

---

admit that the Heustis Gun has a certain ring to it. And Seacow Head would have made a fine centre for the world's armament industry.

A block was a delicate but simple piece of technology. An ironwood pulley — or sheave — was enclosed in a wooden casing. The sheave turned on a wooden or metal axle, and the casing was held together with four bolts. Depending on the load it was expected to lift, the sheaves might be ganged together, with two, three or four nestled side by side in the same casing. The more sheaves your block possessed, the more weight it would lift. If you've ever seen a mechanic's chain hoist in action, you've seen a block at work.

Even the smallest sailing vessel required hundreds of blocks. No sail could be set or adjusted without them. Although sometimes sheaves or axles might be mass-produced, the majority were individually hand crafted. And they had to be replaced frequently, because even ironwood wore out under the stresses of everyday use. Gradually, in the more expensive models, the sheaves, axles and even casings were cast in iron.

Duchemin began to advertise his services as a pump and block maker in the late 1830s. Aside from the occasional runaway apprentice (ungrateful wretches!) his career followed a normal course for a Victorian craftsman. But in the 1850s he began to dabble in ways to improve his product. Intrigued with the possibilities of metal parts, he came upon a way to take his blocks to a whole new level of technology. He invented a roller bearing.

Patented some time in the early 1860s, his idea was to dispense entirely with hanging the sheave on an axle. Instead, why not surround the sheave with a whole bunch of little axles, each precisely the same size to reduce friction when they rubbed together. If you'd like to see a roller bearing in action, tear apart the wheel assembly of your (or preferably somebody else's) car. Right where the bit that rolls on the road meets the bit that's attached to the engine, you ll find a roller bearing assembly. Much like the one Watson Duchemin devised for his patented all-metal block.

Duchemin also demonstrated that he was more than a one-invention wonder. He was interested in the problems inherent in moving eggs from place to place. In one piece. To this end, in 1871, he sent another application off to the patent office. Duchemin's Improved Egg Carrier provided each egg with an individual cloth pocket to ride in. Suspended on a wooden rack, twenty-four of these pockets made a flat. The flats were then arranged so they could be stacked. A box little more than one foot a side could be made to carry a gross of eggs. Safely, and over any distance. Today the pockets are made from cardboard or styrofoam. We call them egg cartons.

Watson Duchemin died in 1872. His impressive career raises a puzzling question. How is it that someone who invented two currently commonplace things didn't become richer than the dreams of Croesus? Or at least isn't better remembered?

Folklore suggests Duchemin didn't care if he made a fortune from his inventions. That, for instance, he declined to take a commercial patent on his egg carton, preferring to see it as his gift to humanity. Perhaps he suffered from the syndrome of simultaneous discovery. The record suggests that other inventors were coming up with similar inventions at the same time. Historians have yet to sort out who invented what first.

I think he simply should have hired a good patent lawyer.

Two Men and A Boat

he Americans' civil war didn't stir much passion on Prince Edward Island. A handful of Islanders cared enough to actually go and fight — mostly for the North. Others had an inbred hatred of the United States and took delight in its descent into chaos. For most, it was no more than an interesting addition to their daily newspaper.

But for some, it was an excellent source of business opportunities.

James Duncan's business was boats: buying, selling, sailing and building. Born in Scotland, "Wee Jamie" emigrated to Orwell and got in early on the shipbuilding boom of the 1840s. At close to seven feet in height, he was, literally, the biggest shipbuilder in the Colony. He also had to his credit the biggest ship ever built on the Island — the 1800-ton *Ethel*, launched in 1856. In 1862 he decided to try his hand at building a steamship and commissioned a modest paddle-wheeler named the *Heather Belle*.

Heather Belle was a pretty little boat. One hundred and twenty feet long, she had a beam of nineteen feet and could sail in as little as seven feet of water. Her 120 horsepower engine was rated at fourteen knots, but was able to deliver seventeen in a pinch. Such speed came at a price — a third of *Heather Belle's* hold was taken by engine and bunker space. But the boat was not intended to compete for large, bulky cargoes. She would make her profits on passenger runs or as a carrier of high-end perishable goods. Or, it gradually dawned on Duncan, possibly as a blockade runner.

With the beginning of the Civil War, the North had clamped a naval blockade on the South. Since the Confederates had no navy to speak of, they were quickly cut off from outside trade. But the blockade had holes in it. There were several thousand miles of coastline to patrol, and there was no shortage of captains willing to try and get through. The profits were huge for those who were clever enough, or lucky enough or fast enough to get their cargo into a Southern port.

On paper, you couldn't have designed a better blockade-runner than *Heather Belle*. With a low profile and no masts, she was almost impossible to spot from a distance. What she couldn't hide from she could outrun — no sail-powered warship could match her speed. What she couldn't outrun she could outmanoeuvre. Drawing so little water, she could leap the shallowest shoals with a single bound. Her small cargo hold had ample room for the kinds of luxury items that fetched much money in wartime. The venture was risky — one unsuccessful encounter with the Union Navy meant the loss of both cargo and carrier. But the possibilities were enticing. A few successful voyages would pay the boat off. Anything after that was pure profit.

One of the Charlottetown residents most aware of these possibilities was James Sherman, Chief American Consul. The Americans had established an official presence on the Island in the 1850s as part of the Reciprocity Treaty — a free trade agreement between the United States and Britain's North American colonies. The treaty allowed American access to the rich fisheries off Prince Edward Island. Consular duties usually centred on soothing the feathers that got ruffled whenever six hundred New England fishing schooners descended on Island ports.

Sherman had only recently arrived on the Island. His predecessor had been a Southerner with suspect loyalties. The posting was a minor one, but he threw himself into his duties with energy. Though winter was traditionally a slack time at the Consulate, he maintained a constant stream of despatches to his superiors in Washington. Politics, weather, crop yields — he dutifully filed information on a range of vital topics. Shortly after New Year's, 1863, his report assumed a frantic tone.

A huge gang of workmen were swarming around James Duncan's new boat. The traditional January thaw had softened the ice, and the workers, armed with ice saws, were cutting a path to the mouth of the harbour. A puzzled Sherman made some inquiries and was appalled by what he heard. Though he'd left it rather late in the season, the story went, Wee Jamie had decided to try his boat against the Union blockade. A variation suggested he was merely trying to get the *Heather Belle* to Halifax, where she would be sold for an outrageous sum. The new owners in turn would put her to work as a blockade-runner. Either way, Sherman reported, a small but nasty thorn for the Union Navy was being prepared. He needed instructions. What should he do? Unfortu-

Heather Belle *was a pretty little boat.*

nately, if he received a reply, it was never filed, so we'll never know how gravely the matter was received in Washington.

As it turned out, the Consul's worries were wasted. As any Islander could have told him, the only thing more inevitable than the January thaw was the cold snap that followed. The cutting crews tried for a week to get *Heather Belle* to open water, but weren't able to compete with the thickening ice. After a particularly hard freeze, Duncan admitted defeat and paid off the workers. *Heather Belle* would spend the winter in Charlottetown after all.

Even so, the *Heather Belle* had a final chance for an exciting life. Perhaps, Sherman wrote the following spring, Washington would like him to buy the boat for the Union Navy? Again, no reply was filed, but given that paddle-wheelers weren't very cannon ball-proof, you can imagine their level of interest. In the end, *Heather Belle* was sold to a local company that needed a river boat.

The stresses of Consular duties proved too much for James Sherman. He took a stroke and died in 1865. Flags in the city flew at half-mast as his coffin was carried down to the harbour. Jamie Duncan continued to build ships until 1878, when the collapse of the industry brought him down in spectacular fashion. (The bigger they are, the harder they etc., etc.) Legend had him led from his office to debtors prison — a great story but probably not true, since we were no longer jailing bankrupt businessmen by 1878. Instead he quietly left the province and returned to his native Scotland, where he died as broke as he began. Once a significant figure in the Island's economy, his death rated a bare two lines in the local papers.

Heather Belle outlived them both. Denied one career as a block-ade-runner, and another as a warship, she settled into a long quiet life as a river steamer. A common sight on the three rivers draining into Charlottetown harbour, her main excitement came from the occasional temperance excursion or overnight trip to Pictou.

Father Belcourt Takes
A Test Drive

I, Jerimiah Peters, of Howlan in Prince County, make oath and say:

That I was born in Rustico, on the 18th of April, 1855.
That I quite distinctly remember Father George A. Belcourt, parish priest of Rustico from 1859 to 1869.
That I remember seeing the steam carriage operated by Father Belcourt. This would be about the year 1866. The carriage appeared to be an ordinary driving carriage propelled with a small steam engine as a source of motive power.

— sworn before a Justice of the Peace,
August 1940

eorge-Antoine Belcourt was born in Quebec in 1803. He studied at a local seminary and was ordained a Catholic priest in 1827.

Belcourt spent most of his career as a missionary among the Métis of what would become Manitoba. He was known as a radical, committed to the cause of full political rights for the Métis people. This made him somewhat worrisome to his superiors in Quebec — and downright annoying to the Hudson's Bay Company, which controlled the lands the Métis lived on. In 1859, when he went east for a vacation, the Company refused to allow him back into its territory. Not wanting to see a good priest go to waste, the Bishop of Quebec offered him to the Bishop of Charlottetown.

Arriving in the small fishing village of Rustico, Father Belcourt was soon making his presence felt in his new parish. He was the driving force behind the formation of the Farmers' Bank of Rustico — the smallest bank ever chartered in Canada. He used some impressive connections in France to persuade Emperor Napoleon III to grant a 1,000 franc annuity to start a parish school and library — this at a time when his Bishop couldn't get the Colonial government to grant a thin nickel to the same cause. Ironically, in the midst of this impressive resumé, he's best remembered for a fairly minor incident in his career.

In 1866 he happened to visit a carriage builder in New Jersey. The builder was experimenting with a self-propelled vehicle by installing a small steam engine on an ordinary driving buggy. The result, though odd-looking, intrigued Belcourt. His parish was large and he had to do a lot of travelling. Just think of the money he'd save on oats and blacksmiths if he could eliminate the horse from the carriage. He bought one and had it shipped back to Rustico. It arrived in late December 1866. The first horseless carriage ever imported into British North America.

The country's first imported car. And its first car accident.

His parishioners weren't impressed. "It'll never work," forecast some. "If it does work, it'll scare the horses," warned others. Father Belcourt was undaunted. On St. Jean Baptiste Day, 1867, the vehicle was formally presented at the parish picnic. After the crowd had their chance to view and admire, Belcourt prepared to give them their first look at a horseless carriage in action.

"Light a fire under the boiler," he ordered his housekeeper. "No," he amended as he saw smoke curling up from the ground beneath the vehicle. "I meant light a fire in the *firebox* under the boiler." Soon the engine was brought up to steam. Father Belcourt climbed aboard, opened his throttle and, to the astonishment and delight of his parishioners, roared off down the highway.

No one was ever sure exactly *how* he ended up wrapped around the fence of an adjacent field. It may have been that the vehicle's builder didn't think the thing might need brakes. Or simply forgot to install them. It may have been that Father Belcourt, in his excitement — or terror — didn't see the bend in the road until he'd gone past it. Whatever the cause, he made history three times that day. The country's first imported car. Its first car driver. And its first car accident.

Father Belcourt was unhurt but chastened by the experience. He swore off horseless carriages and returned to a mode of transportation that had more sense than to run into a fence. The carriage itself was past repair, but the steam engine apparently found employment at a local sawmill.

In later years the Island maintained an uneasy relationship with the automobile. In the early 1900s, as horseless carriages became a common sight, the Legislature took stern measures to limit their use. They were only gradually, grudgingly allowed onto the roads. As late as 1917 there were stretches of highway closed to automobiles.

After motor vehicles were allowed on the roads, Islanders began to work on their reputation as bad drivers. In 1928, a distraught *Guardian* admitted: "Experienced drivers have told us more than once that they feel safer in the streets of Boston or New York, than in Charlottetown." Even today, our general rule of the road has been described as: "Hesitate, then do the completely unexpected." But now, at least you can see that it's not entirely our fault.

We got off to a bad start.

P. John Burden

The Hanging of George Dowie

ownal Square is in the west end of Charlottetown. Graced by gorgeous elm trees, it's a quiet place. Indeed, you'll find a municipal playground there. But in the 1800s this is where the city jail was. And, when needed, the gallows. The latter gives Pownal Square a place in national history. For this is where one of the last public hangings in Canada took place.

In the British era, the Island's first death sentence was passed in 1778. A servant named Elizabeth Mukely was sentenced to hang for stealing £7.7 from her employer. When the court could find no one in the colony willing to execute a woman, the sentence was commuted to banishment.

The first actual death penalty came in 1792, when a man named Cash was hanged for rape. As in the rest of the Empire, the Colony had a range of offenses punishable by death. Getting caught in a serious crime like rape or murder, of course, could get you hanged. But so could break and enter, or some forms of petty theft. It might sound Dickensian, but in 1813 a man was hanged in Charlottetown for stealing a loaf of bread. (Legend has it that he could have received clemency, but the fact he didn't eat the crust was proof he didn't even *need* the bread.) In an era with no organized police forces, the community hoped that the ultimate penalty would serve as the ultimate deterrent to crime. Public execution — "pour encourager les autres" — was the tradition.

By the 1860s there was a movement afoot in the Colonies to move state executions indoors. Some of the softer-hearted citizenry argued they could live without the lessons offered by a public hanging. On the Island, where the death penalty was not used that frequently, the issue seemed moot. Until the hanging of George Dowie.

George Dowie was a sailor, and Charlottetown was an occasional port of call for him. He lived hard. "During all my voyages, and when I was in port," he later confessed, "there was no sin of which I was not guilty." While in Charlottetown, he preferred to stay at the house of a "female acquaintance." He was at this house one night when he and another man got into an argument over a woman. They were both drunk. Dowie settled the argument by stabbing his debating partner in the chest. The latter died and Dowie, caught in the act, was arrested. After a short trial he was found guilty and sentenced to hang. Routine appeals for clemency were sent to the Colonial Office, where they were refused. On April 6, 1869, the Governor was instructed, George Dowie was to die as sentenced.

The Island's last public hanging was one to remember. "Regard for the feelings of our readers restrains us," a disgusted *Islander* reported, "from giving publicly the manner in which the sentence of the court was executed on this poor criminal. The details are far too revolting to be either recorded or read." Fortunately for us blood-thirsty historians, rival papers like the *Patriot* were not so squeamish.

At half-past noon Dowie was taken from his jail cell to the gallows. A crowd of fifteen hundred, gathering since 11:00 a.m., was on hand to watch. Twenty volunteers from the City Militia were on hand to mount a guard. They were nervous. As Dowie came into view, some wag in the crowd shouted: "Rescue him!" When the Guard whirled about, bayonets fixed, joking ceased.

In accordance with tradition, Dowie had a hearty last meal. He'd also had a recent religious conversion, and was calm as he climbed the scaffold. His last statement consisted of eight closely written pages and a seventeen-stanza poem dedicated to his mother and wife. The authorities provided him with an armchair to sit in while he read.

He confessed the sins of a misspent life, described his recent conversion to Christ and urged others like him to avoid the "drink, vicious inclinations, evil habits, and dens of iniquity" that brought him to his present situation. After reading for half an hour, he was done. Standing up, he thanked the Clergymen who had come to pray for him, thanked his lawyers for trying their best, told the executioner he had no hard feelings, and then turned to face the rope. The executioner fixed the noose. The trap door swung open. Dowie plunged through. The rope broke.

It was fifteen feet to the ground. The crowd buzzed with confusion as horrified officials rushed to the dazed Dowie, gathered him up and hustled him into the nearby Jail. When he regained consciousness, Dowie at first thought the whole thing was over and that he was dead. When he was told he was still alive, he thought a last-minute order for clemency had come through. Even after he was told the truth, he remained calm. Back at the gallows, the executioner and his assistants frantically rigged another rope.

An hour later Dowie was returned to the scaffold. Since he was too shaken to walk, his jailers carried him up the stairs in a chair. Once again the noose was fixed. Once again George Dowie plunged through the trap door. Once again he hit the ground.

This time it was a broken cleat.

As the crowd surged forward to see what was happening and the militia strained to push them back, the executioner summoned his assistants and they hoisted the condemned by hand. Dowie was so still that some thought he must have been killed by the second fall. Probably he was simply too stunned to struggle. After fifteen minutes he was cut down, pronounced dead and hastily carted off to a nearby cemetery.

Despite what he had done to warrant the punishment, the quiet calm and dignity with which George Dowie faced his demise stood in stark contrast to the horrific manner of that death. "In the name of our common humanity, which had been so terribly outraged," summed up the *Patriot*, "let our people resolve that a public execution shall never again take place in this colony."

Orange Day
in July

t's hard to imagine the passion and fury inherent in a piece of yellow cloth. But late last century, when the cloth was made into a flag and flown on the 12th of July, it became a symbol of triumph and righteousness for some — oppression and hatred for others.

The yellow flag belonged to the Loyal Order of the Orange Lodge. The 12th of July was the anniversary of the Battle of the Boyne, when Protestant William III (King Billy) crushed once and for all the forces of Roman Catholicism in Great Britain. Or, at least, that's what the Protestants liked to believe.

The Orange Lodge was originally a secret society dedicated to ensuring the Catholics stayed good and crushed. It came to the Island in the 1860s amidst much angry debate. But here it was as much a social club as an agent of oppression. Still, every year on the 12th of July, when that yellow flag flew above Orange Halls throughout the province, Catholics were reminded that some of their neighbours regarded them as inferior and not altogether trustworthy.

That wasn't very nice.

Despite these undercurrents, Orange parades in Charlottetown tended to be fairly low-key. Thursday the 12th, 1877, started off like that. About 150 Orangemen embarked on a chartered steamer and sailed up the West River for a day of picnicking, games and good fellowship. Around seven that evening they came back to town, formed up at the wharf and paraded back to their Hall on Queen Street.

It was right around this time that all hell broke loose.

A large crowd had gathered on the street opposite the Orange Hall. They were mostly spectators, but a few taunts and jeers were heard as the Orangemen raised their yellow flag and filed in for their meeting. Inside, the Glorious 12th celebrations wrapped up with a few speeches and the members got ready to go home. Outside, twenty or thirty angry onlookers — all, it was alleged, Irishmen — stared at the flag in sullen and, possibly, drunken hatred.

Queen Street was being paved that summer. Piles of fist-sized stones — ideal for throwing — were lying everywhere. As the Orangemen began to exit, some of these rocks began to fly toward their Hall. One Orangeman, obviously prepared for every eventuality, drew a pistol from his pocket and answered the stone throwers with a single shot.

It was right around this time that all hell broke loose.

As the spectators ran for cover, the Street Rowdies (as they were labelled later) hurled a volley of pavers. The Orangemen fell back into the Hall. A few who were carrying revolvers manned the windows and began firing at the crowd. The Rowdies seemed undeterred by bullets. They fell back when the Orangemen were shooting, then rushed forward with more stones while they were reloading. The few policemen present stood aside, dumbfounded. The Orange leaders — Senator Haviland and Dr. Jenkins — screamed in the din for everyone to cut it out. After several minutes of pure chaos, the battle reached a natural lull.

The Orangemen must have been: a) very careful to fire over the crowd's head, b) God-awful marksmen or, c) incredibly lucky. No one was killed in the gunfire, but several bystanders were wounded — one bullet had grazed a man's temple. While the two sides contemplated their next moves, the ranking policemen on the scene arranged a hasty truce.

The Rowdies said they would leave quietly, if the Orangemen lowered the hated yellow flag. After some persuasion the flag began to come down, but when the Orangemen heard the Rowdies cheering, they got mad and raised it up again. More rocks flew toward the Hall, and the Orangemen were preparing another round of gunfire when the police convinced them to lower the flag for good. Considering the victory theirs, the Rowdies marched off as promised, singing and chanting in celebration. Shocked and angry, the Orangemen also went home. The fighting had stopped, but no one thought the battle was over.

Disgusted by the victory of the Mob, and dismayed by the inaction of the police, many felt Charlottetown had been given over to a gang of lawless hooligans. Another confrontation seemed inevitable. There was a run on revolvers in local hardware stores as the City braced itself for Friday the 13th.

The next day the Orangemen marched defiantly back to their Hall. They met, made speeches, passed strong resolutions and raised their yellow flag again. The Rowdies, hoping for a rematch, were waiting for them.

So was a company of militia cavalry.

So were the police — bolstered by a hundred hastily sworn-in constables. Before a single stone could be hefted, or pistol cocked, they put an end to the proceedings by arresting every Rowdie in sight and bundling them off to jail.[1]

The aftermath of the riot generated surprisingly little bitterness between the two communities. The Catholic establishment, though it regretted the Orange Lodge's insistence on holding its odious annual parade, defended its right to do so unmolested. The riot had been the work of corner loafers and street ruffians, and no self-respecting Catholic could condone their actions. The Protestant establishment, for its part, condemned the fools on the Orange side who had been so quick to open fire with their sidearms. Ironically, the riot may have served to bring the two communities closer together.

What a difference a decade makes!

If the Orange Riot had occurred in, say, 1867, the outcome would have been very different. Then, the Colony's Catholics regarded the Orange Lodge as a sinister cabal openly plotting their destruction. Likewise, the Colony's Protestants were convinced many of their Catholic neighbours were closet Fenians just waiting for the right time to rise up and murder them in their beds. Given the temper of that time, an Orange Riot might easily have turned into a running gun battle fought through the streets of Charlottetown. As it was, it can be considered the last real battle in the Island's wars of religion. Though they reserved the right to mislike and mistrust each other well into the following century, Protestants and Catholics resisted the temptation to employ rocks, axe handles and pistols in their theological discourses.

---

[1] Throwing stones at a lawful assembly was apparently an arrestable offence. Replying to the stone throwers with pistol fire was, apparently, not.

Riches to Rags: James and Edith Peake

Wealthy, handsome, well turned out and impeccably connected, James and Edith Peake were the Island's aristocracy. They were born with every advantage and lived with magnificent flair. And their story had an ending as tragic as a gooey Gothic novel.

Prince Edward Island blossomed in the 1850s and '60s. Aside from a few nasty political issues, the Colony had never known better times. The economy was strong, buoyed by its booming shipyards and a free trade treaty with the United States. The hard scrabble settlements of "pioneer" days had been displaced by tight, tidy farm communities. Citizens revelled in the semi-independence brought by responsible government. Energy and confidence abounded. It was the Island's "Golden Age."

James Peake was a perfect representative for the era. His father, James Sr., came to the Island in the 1820s. The elder Peake was a prosperous merchant and shipbuilder with 152 vessels to his credit. James Jr. was born in 1842. As the eldest son, he stood to inherit the bulk of the business his father built.

As was the custom among well-born young men, James and his brothers George and Ralph were educated in England. Though his schoolmasters in England despaired over his lack of scholarly aptitude, James had few worries. His inheritance was large and he looked gorgeous in a uniform — a well-born young Englishman in the 1860s needed little else.

After their father's death in 1860, James and his brothers took over the family business. Within a few years, Peake Brothers was one of the largest firms on the Island. They required three quays on the Charlottetown waterfront to handle their mercantile business. Their shipyards were among the busiest in the Colony. The vessels they launched had an admirable reputation, often fetching double the average price for Island-built vessels. Rich, charming and handsome, James Peake was the Colony's most eligible bachelor in the mid-1860s.

In 1864 he met Edith Haviland. Edith came from one of the Colony's most prominent political families. Her father, Thomas Heath, was a Tory powerbroker who would be remembered as a Father of Confederation and Lieutenant Governor. The Havilands were connected, through family and favour, to most of the Colony's social and business elite. The courtship quickly turned serious — in 1865 a beautiful, 250-ton brig named the *Edith Haviland* came down the slipway at one of the Peake shipyards.[1] In 1866 the Anglican Bishop for Halifax officiated at their marriage. In Victorian style, their first child followed a year later — their second a year after that.

The Island's economy continued to boom through the 1860s, but slumped in the early '70s. Peake Brothers rode out the recession under the leadership of young Ralph, who the family agreed had the best head for business. When good times returned in the mid-70s, the firm recorded some admirable profits. James himself drew a yearly salary of $3,000 — roughly ten times the average working wage. What with their family growing, and business doing so well, James and Edith decided to build a home that reflected their success.

They called it Beaconsfield, after Benjamin Disraeli, Earl of Beaconsfield — a British politician whom James particularly admired. Though not overly large, it was the grandest house on the Island. The Peakes hired a hot young architect named William C. Harris, told him to pull out all the stops and gave him a blank cheque. His design brimmed with the latest conveniences — hot and cold running water, central heat, indoor plumbing and gas light. The finish was luxurious and the location, on the harbour and next to the Governor's residence, was the envy of the neighbourhood. The final bill was somewhere around $50,000.

---

[1] The figurehead for *Edith H* was a well-endowed, scantily attired woman. Shipbuilders enjoyed some unique opportunities for getting a gal's attention.

To give an idea of how much money $50,000 was in 1875, here are some comparisons. An ordinary house, equivalent to our modern-day bungalow, could be built for $500 to $1,000. Five thousand dollars could put you into something *really* nice. At any of the Peake shipyards, $50,000 would have bought you a half-dozen brigs and a couple of full-rigged ships — an entire deep-sea shipping fleet. Province House, the grandest public building in the Maritimes, had cost around $85,000 to finish in 1850. By any standards, Beaconsfield was an expensive house. By Island standards, its like had never been seen before.

In 1877 the Peake family moved into their magnificent new home. They enjoyed entertaining and there were probably few invitations more sought after. Especially after the Vice-Regal visit of 1879, when James and Edith hosted the Princess Louise and her husband, the Marquis of Lorne. It was no surprise that Beaconsfield was included in the itinerary. James was, after all, an Aide-de-Camp to the Lieutenant Governor. And his son-in-law.

It was the grandest house on the Island.

Princess Louise was a daughter of Queen Victoria. The Marquis of Lorne was serving as Canada's Governor General. They were a much-loved, deliciously flamboyant couple and Charlottetown hadn't been so excited over a Royal Visit since 1860, when Louise's brother, Prince Albert, came to call. To the delight of the Charlottetown press, the Royals had such a good time at the Peakes' place they were late for their official reception, up the lane at Government house. In a society that set great store in social standing, James and Edith Peake had reached a pinnacle.

After 1879, the Peakes' fairy tale quickly turned to melodrama. The following summer a diphtheria epidemic killed two of their children. Business worries compounded personal tragedy. A world-wide depression set its grip on the Island economy. Ralph Peake, who'd pulled Peake Brothers through earlier recessions, had died suddenly the year before. Worse than the loss of Ralph's expertise, the firm's foundation — shipbuilding — went into a sudden slump. Shipbuilders assumed it was simply a temporary downturn. It was, instead, the beginning of the end for the industry. The Bank of Prince Edward Island collapsed. As a governor, James was on the hook for a great deal of liability to the depositors. Finally, as if to symbolize the mounting disasters, one of the biggest vessels in the Peake fleet, the barque *James Peake*, sank in an Atlantic storm. It was not insured.

The Peakes, of course, were not alone in their economic woes. In the early 1880s, the Island embarked on one of the worst depressions in its history. For all the blows they endured, James and Edith might have been able to weather the storm — many others did. But the Peakes had Beaconsfield, and it was their undoing.

The house had been built with mostly borrowed money. In 1881, several huge notes came due. In normal times, this would not have been a problem. James would have simply drawn an advance from the business. But the business was fighting for survival, and James couldn't even offer to pay the interest due. His creditors had problems of their own, and at the first whiff of insolvency, they swept in to grab what they could. To protect itself, Peake Brothers bought James out — a formality only, because when James' debts were tallied against his assets in the firm, he ended up owing *it* money. He declared bankruptcy in 1882. The golden age had ended.

James and Edith Peake were penniless.

On moving out of Beaconsfield, Edith took the surviving children to live with her parents. They, apparently, were willing to support their unfortunate daughter, but not her humiliated husband. James took a room in one of the cheaper neighbourhoods. It's amazing how few his friends became, once he lost his fortune. By 1888 he decided he would not be able to rebuild on the Island, so he went west. He tried his hand at bookkeeping in Minnesota, then drifted to Victoria, British Columbia. There he tried to set himself up as a liquor merchant, but failed in several successive ventures. Eighteen ninety-five found him employed as a billiard marker at a local Gentlemen's Club.

"I am very sorry that I cannot send you a present this time," he wrote his son, Lorne, who had been born a year after that glorious party at Beaconsfield. "As you know, dear boy, that I have been for some time out of work, but I shall not forget you when I make some money. I have got to work with Mr. Anderson, and am now writing this in a dark cellar and can hardly see to write.

"I received a nice letter from your very dear Mother yesterday," he continued. "I am very glad to hear you are quite well. You will soon be getting your summer holidays and I hope you will pass good examinations, my dear boy, and carry off some prizes. Continue to be good and kind to your dearest Mother, and kiss her for Papa. God bless and watch over you, my dear son. Goodbye." The letter was dated June 18, 1895. Three weeks later, James Peake suffered "a paralysis of the brain," and died. He was fifty-three.

James Peake and Edith Haviland were the golden children of a golden era. Ironically, the one thing they didn't possess was that which came naturally to poorer folk — the ability to survive unexpected hardship. When their world came crashing down they found themselves, like children, bewildered and helpless. Like characters in an overly moralistic novel, they lived lives everyone must have envied, and came to an end anyone would have dreaded.

Sometimes, the Phoenix Doesn't Rise

uilt in 1879, HMS *Phoenix* was a hybrid. At first glance, she might have passed for a traditional warship. Her gundeck was laid out in the age-old manner, with a row of cannon lining each side of the hull. Also in keeping with tradition, she was sail powered, although her masts were short and ugly. But poking up between two of the masts was a funnel for the steam engine below decks, and her hull was made entirely of iron. Like so many of her sisters, the eleven-hundred-ton gunboat was an experiment in blending old technologies with new.

In September 1882 the *Phoenix* was on its way from Quebec City to Halifax. Her commander, Captain Hubert Herbert Grenfell, was planning to shave a day off the voyage by sailing through the Strait of Canso, shunning the safer route around Cape Breton. Aside from the narrow passage through Canso, the only tricky bit of navigation involved was around East Point. Here the Gulf of St. Lawrence met the Northumberland Strait, and the treacherous winds and tides generated could make for a miserable passage — especially for sailing vessels. But Grenfell was confident. He had the option of making the passage under power, and as long as he took care to avoid the reef that reached out two miles from shore, there could be no possibility of trouble.

It was nighttime — dark and stormy — as HMS *Phoenix* approached the Point. She was under sail — naval officers still preferred sailpower, both to demonstrate their seamanship and conserve coal. Before going to bed, Captain Grenfell checked the course against his charts. His calculations suggested *Phoenix* would clear the reef with miles to spare. For extra insurance, the helmsman would be able to use the lighthouse beacon to judge his distance from shore. As a precaution against the weather, Grenfell ordered the sails be shortened. Then he retired for the night. A few hours later he awoke to the worst sound he could have imagined — eleven hundred tons of metal hitting a rock reef at close to full speed.

HMS Phoenix *was now part of East Point reef.*

At first, there was no reason to panic. Although the warship was fully aground, her watertight compartments would keep her from sinking. When the time was right, her powerful steam engine should have been able to pull her out of danger. All Grenfell had to do was wait for light and a high tide, and *Phoenix* should be able to back off the reef. But the storm and heavy seas continued to rise. With daylight came a low tide. *Phoenix* was high and dry, and the waves soon smashed her exposed propeller to scrap. Worse, so many watertight compartments were torn open that, when the high tide returned, Grenfell found his command three-quarters full of water. His thoughts turned to getting the crew off safely.

Phoenix struck late on a Tuesday night. It was Thursday before the weather eased enough to launch the lifeboats. With the help of local fishermen, Grenfell managed to get his hundred-man crew ashore without mishap. They brewed up some cocoa and thanked their lucky stars. He went to look for a telegraph to tell the Admiralty he'd just lost one of their warships.

It wasn't every day that a major man-of-war was lost at sea. The *Phoenix* quickly became a major news story — it even rated an engraving in the *London Graphic*. The main angle? Would the *Phoenix* rise again?

Three vessels were sent from Halifax to see if the vessel could be salvaged. They took off everything they could, including six heavy cannon and one of those newfangled Gatling guns. *Phoenix* wouldn't budge. A crew of local lads tried to help by removing a very heavy keg of rum. This didn't help *Phoenix* much, but there was a fine party in the sand dunes. Grenfell and his officers turned a blind eye, considering a keg of Her Majesty's rum small payment for the risks the locals had taken in getting the crew safely ashore.

After a month, as the winter weather began to set in, the Navy conceded that *Phoenix* was a write-off. One of the world's most advanced warships, barely three years out of the shipyard, was sold as scrap for

It wasn't every day that a major man-of-war was lost at sea.

£3,000. The Quebec Wrecking Company came, cut it into manageable pieces and shipped it away.

Losing the *Phoenix* was not good for Hubert Grenfell's career. He still couldn't see what had gone wrong. He checked his charts, then he checked his course, then he double-checked both. He followed all the proper procedures, gave all the right orders, and still his command ended up on the reef. He just didn't understand. The Court of Inquiry didn't care. It found him negligent and issued a reprimand. Although the penalty might have been much worse, the finding effectively ended his naval career. Before the accident he was well on the path of promotion to Admiral. Six years later, only forty-three years old, he resigned from the Navy.

Perhaps he should have summoned a few East Pointers to testify on his behalf. They'd known for years about the dangerous flaw in the navigational aids at East Point. The lighthouse, you see, was in the wrong spot. The Admiralty's charts placed it at the very tip of the Point. It had actually been built a half-mile further down the coast. For navigators relying on the light at night, it was just enough to turn a close but safe course around the reef into a trip right onto the rocks. *Phoenix* wasn't the first vessel to discover this. But it was the most famous. And possibly the last. A year later, the East Point lighthouse was lifted up and dragged to where the charts said it was.

The Wreck of the Tunstall

ome shipwrecks are more embarrassing than tragic. Take, for instance, the tale of the SS *Tunstall*.

The *Tunstall* was a state-of-the-art steamship. Over two hundred feet long, the powerful, steel-hulled steamer was barely four years old. On May 3, 1883, she left Pictou, Nova Scotia, with a load of coal. It was her first voyage of the season, and she was bound for Montreal.

1883 was an especially bad year for ice.

For the first day or so, *Tunstall* made fine progress. But as she neared East Point she found pack ice — as far as the eye could see. Captain Mackie decided to try his luck to the south, but a day later he ran into the same ice pack at Cape Traverse. There seemed no choice but to turn around and set course again for East Point.

The next two days were spent in ice and fog, bouncing alternately between north and south headings. Sailing south near Georgetown, *Tunstall* encountered another steamer, SS *Benona*, and the two decided to team up until they could find their way to clear water. Together, they finally found a path around East Point, and some time during the night *Benona* actually found a lead and sailed to safety. All *Tunstall* found was more ice. Come morning she found herself all alone, with no place to turn.

Steel-hulled vessels like Tunstall had a few advantages when it came to dealing with ice. Unlike its wooden counterparts, *Tunstall* could bump into the occasional ice pan and be little worse for wear. Free from a reliance on sail power, she could weave a path through the pans when heavy ice was present. Or beat a retreat to clear water. But she was not meant to stay in close, intimate company with an entire ice field. On May 12, after the ice closed in and cut off *Tunstall's* last avenues of retreat, the steamer's fate was sealed.

It was somewhere off Covehead, Captain Mackie reckoned, "We got nipped in that tight that the ship began to list. Ice was piling over the rails. It looked as like she would be buried. Next the plates on the starboard side gave way, and the water came in rapidly."

The crew went below and began to shovel the cargo over the side. After shifting a few tons, they discovered where the water was coming from. The ice had punched a two-foot hole in the hull. It was plugged for the time being, but the Captain felt sure that as soon as the ice plug was pulled, *Tunstall* had no place to go but down. He ordered the lifeboats lowered.

Here, in the gathering dusk, the only fatality of the Tunstall *occurred.*

It must have been very embarrassing, getting yourself sunk by ice, in the middle of May, in the warmest waters north of Florida. But it did have its advantages. No one was in danger of being drown'd in a storm toss'd sea. Everyone had time to gather up their gear. After the boats were launched, nobody had to row. They just hitched up a couple of ropes and hauled them a safe distance away. Shortly after this was done the ice shifted and water began to pour into *Tunstall's* hold. Late that afternoon the crew stood by their lifeboats and watched *Tunstall* dip her nose under the ice and slide to the bottom.

Here, in the gathering dusk, the only fatality of the *Tunstall* incident occurred. The future was uncertain. It was foggy, and no one knew how far offshore they were. Or what direction the ice was drifting. Or how long it would be until they might find themselves safely ashore. Included in *Tunstall's* deck cargo were two live pigs. It seemed silly to risk a possible death by malnutrition with two lovely pigs among the ship's complement. They were slaughtered and set to chill by the boats. Just in case. This done, the crew settled down to a night on the ice.

Monday morning dawned clear. The ice field had drifted close to shore, and the Captain realized they might simply walk to safety. Leaving the boats they struck off on foot. By Monday evening they scrambled ashore by the lighthouse at the mouth of St. Peter's Bay.

Three of the crew, however, had to take a more roundabout way to safety. As seaman James Crock remembered: "We were just in hailing distance of the shore when the ice separated, and the Second Mate, the Cook and myself got separated from the Captain and the rest of the crew." Cut off from shore, the three had no choice but to return to the lifeboats. Here they built a fire and the Cook made himself useful by cooking the two pigs. They laid their pork store in one of the boats and settled in for their second night on the ice.

On Tuesday morning the three found enough open water to launch their boat, and they spent the day rowing through the thick fog and ice cakes. They obviously had no idea where they were going, because later that afternoon a Cable Head farmer named MacKenzie spotted them heading roughly in the direction of the Atlantic Ocean. MacKenzie rallied his sons and neighbours, launched his dory, and brought the last of the *Tunstall* crew safely ashore.

At this point, the wreck of the *Tunstall* took a mysterious turn. After bringing Mr. Crock and his mates to safety, MacKenzie and his neighbours headed back out, no doubt looking to reward their good deed with a bit of salvage from the wreck. They found nothing. There were later attempts to locate the wreck off the mouth of the harbour, where the rest of the crew came ashore. Again, nothing was found. Then the salvagers realized they had no way of knowing how far the drifting ice had carried the crew after their ship went down. The Captain had been too busy before she went down to take a navigational fix, and she'd been too far offshore to see any landmarks. SS *Tunstall* was lost in the purest sense of the word.

By the 1930s, fishermen off Covehead were noticing that a certain spot on their lobster grounds was notorious for snagging gear. They also found that the lobsters they caught there had a black tinge to their shells, and their drags often brought up lumps of coal. They realized they were fishing over a wreck and dubbed it "the Coal Boat." Those who remembered the *Tunstall* realized that this was where she went down.

The wreck is still there. You can even visit it, if you want to. All you need is some good scuba gear and someone who happens to know the Loran co-ordinates. But if there are ice pans in the vicinity, remember the *Tunstall* rule.

Ice and water craft don't mix.

Ice Follies

A vast bank, apparently a couple of hundred feet high, white, shrouded with snow to the summit, presented a few, glistening angles to the setting sun, which sank angry, red and sullen in the west behind Bay Verte. "This then," I said, "is the Island?" "Island," snorted my informant, "what you see is not four miles off. Cape Traverse is nigh upon ten. That is a mass of bergs which have come down this afternoon with the tide from the north." "Heavens," I muttered, "have I to cross this hideous Rubicon?

— B.W.A. Sleigh, 1852

n January 1850, Archie Campbell of Lot 27 was on his way home from a trip to the mainland. When he got to Cape Tormentine he discovered he'd missed the iceboat. It was a nice day, so he grabbed a fencepost — just in case he fell through — and set out on foot. That was around one in the afternoon. By dusk, he was safely ashore at Cape Traverse.

Sometimes, it was that easy.

On March 10, 1855, an iceboat set out from Cape Tormentine for Cape Traverse. When they set out the weather was fine, but, "After crossing without incident to within a half mile of the Island shore, a storm of sleet and snow grew violent, and the lolly lay so deep they could not force the boat through it."

Lolly was the name given to the confused state where salt water can't decide whether to stay liquid or freeze solid. Too soft to walk on, too solid to row through, lolly was the bane of the iceboats. With dusk approaching, this crew admitted defeat and turned back to solid ice. When it got too dark to go on, they turned the boat on its side and spent a long, cold night on the ice.

Morning found them further from both shores — ice in the North-umberland Strait tends to drift southeast, where the strait is wider. An-other full day's trekking still had them on the ice. Another night in the open found them utterly exhausted. One of the passengers, a young man named Hazard, was too weak to go on. The time had come for desperate measures.

"Fortunately Mr. Weir," the paper later reported, "had with him a small spaniel which they killed, *drank its blood, and passengers and crew ate the flesh. Raw!*[1] This revived them." They then set all their luggage on the ice (except, of course, for the mail), bundled Hazard into the boat, and pressed on. They came ashore the next morning near Pugwash, Nova Scotia — about a half a day too late for Henry Hazard, who had died during the night.

Sometimes, it was that brutal.

The iceboats were instituted in the reign of Governor Patterson as a method to get mail — and really determined passengers — across the Northumberland Strait in wintertime. They were simple craft — light rowboats with iron strips running along each side of the keel and a leather shoulder harness by each oarlock. They were simple to operate. In open water, the crew rowed. Whenever they came to a pan or pack of ice, they jumped out, slung the harness over their shoulders, and pulled the boat along the ice. On coming to open water, they jumped back in and rowed until they found more ice to run on. Passengers had the op-tion of sitting in with the mail or running along with the crew. The incentive to run with the boat was twofold. One, the fare was cheaper. Two, it kept you warm.

Though always dangerous, the majority of crossings fell somewhere between the ease of Archie Cameron's afternoon stroll and the night-mare of the 1855 tragedy. The best/only description of an iceboat cross-ing was set down by the celebrated Colonel Sleigh.

Sleigh made his crossing in the winter of 1852. On arriving at Tormentine he contacted Captain Irving, who commanded the iceboat. After some thought, he decided to run with the boat, instead of sitting like a piece of baggage.

The ice in the Strait comes in a variety of forms. Wind and tide push it back and forth, pushing up high ridges here, pulling out smooth patches there. Close to shore, where the ice actually touched bottom,

---

[1] Victorian newspapers only ever used italics *to denote extreme shock and horror.*

The time had come for desperate measures.

boulder fields and pressure ridges were inevitable. But not insurmountable.

> as a long ridge of sharp boulders had to be escaladed... Captain Irving sprang forward with a line, and clambered up a mass of ice some 15 feet high. He got up on the other side, and all hands applying full strength, we pushed the boat up after him. A couple of the crew now mounted on the top of the ice, and getting the bows of the boat well poised, they overbalanced her, and down she glided on the other side. I found it a most difficult task to follow these nimble fellows....

As a matter of fact, as he became familiar "with the ups and downs of the journey," Sleigh found the going kind of fun.

After clambering up a boulder, I found the easiest way to gain the other side was to slide down on my back. This in some instances became a dangerous experiment, as, in the gullies between two masses of ice, snow had generally collected to a depth of several feet, and, after going down a rather steep declivity, I found myself up to the armpits in ice, snow and water. Irving being near, he snatched at me, otherwise I ran a fair chance of disappearing. This rendered me more cautious in my sliding experiments.

After several hours of wrestling the boat up ridge and down gully, they were finally clear of the shore ice.

... we had an opportunity to look upon the Straits. Further than the eye could see were enormous fields of ice, with black patches and streaks here and there, appearing like ink from the contrast of the whiteness around. This was the water.

Sleigh got to rest as the crew rowed across the open water. They soon came upon a flat pan of ice. Hauling the boat up, they put their passenger into his harness and began to jog.

While running at full speed, I felt the surface beneath me give way, and with a loud shout from all, the boat sank. In an instant we were struggling up to our shoulders in the water and broken ice. Now the utility of the strap was manifest — it kept us tied to the boat and saved our being plunged into the foaming mass of broken ice and sucked under by the current. Irving in an instant manfully disengaged himself and clambered into the boat. Then cautioning all to remain still, he drew us, one by one, out of the water, drenched to the skin.

The intensity of the cold I shall never forget. It chilled me to my very heart. My clothes became in an instant stiff and frozen. Had it not been for a glass of raw brandy, twice repeated, all round, nothing, I verily believe, could have caused our congealed blood to circulate again through our torpid veins.

Thus, by a series of dunkings and dashes, you crafted a passage across the Strait. It wasn't elegant, but for the better part of 140 years, it was the only reliable winter link with the mainland. Even after the arrival of the "winter" steamers in the 1870s, the iceboats were still routinely called upon. And, despite the unfortunate incident of 1855, their safety record was remarkable. In thousands of voyages over fifteen decades, only two people ever died on an iceboat crossing. Young Mr. Hazard and, ironically, a crewman who drowned just two months before the service ended for good.

The last crossing took place, without fanfare, in April 1917.

The Tunnel

he sense of relief was outweighed only by anger. In January 1885, the Island came within a whisker of its worst iceboat disaster ever. A trio of boats — twenty-two passengers and crew — had set out on a routine crossing. But a sudden storm blew up, cutting them off from shore and stranding them on the ice for two days. Though no one died, the final price for safety included a variety of fingers and toes lost to frostbite, and several cases of pneumonia. It might have been much worse.

Nevertheless, Islanders were shocked and appalled. It was supposed to be an age of progress. You could cross the continent by train in two weeks. Cross the Atlantic by steamship in one. Your telegram to someone on the other side of the world travelled at close to the speed of light — or at least at the speed of electricity. Yet, if it was wintertime, and you wanted to get to or from Prince Edward Island, chances were you'd have to jog across, using a flimsy rowboat to keep from drowning or freezing to death.

There had to be a better way.

The Island did have the services of a winter steamship — subsidized by the Dominion Government. The *Northern Light*, launched in 1875, had been specially designed to brave the ice pack. Her stout hull simply bounced off icebergs that would sink a lesser ship. Her powerful engines could even push the occasional ice pan aside. But experience had taught the *Northern Light* to run from the bigger bergs and stay strictly clear of the thicker ice pack. This, compounded by chronic engine problems, meant the winter steamer usually spent more time at the dock than in the Strait. The lower-tech but more reliable iceboats were often called on to fill in.

It was supposed to be an age of progress.

The near-disaster brought forward a flood of ideas. Go to the root of the problem, an MLA suggested in the House. Put a dam across the Strait of Belle Isle, which separates Newfoundland from Labrador. Not only would this keep Arctic ice out of the Gulf of St. Lawrence, it should also considerably shorten the length of our winter!

Build a huge, pontoon bridge, was another suggestion, and run trains across it. A pontoon bridge would simply float on top of the icepack. What would happen when the pack began to drift was a detail that never got worked out.

What the Island needed, suggested a more pragmatic camp, was a bigger, better winter steamer. Maybe one with huge steam hammers coming out of the bow, to pulverize the ice. Or perhaps a series of bow-mounted propellers, to grind a path through the ice. Or even one with extremely powerful engines and a heavy bow. Any ice it couldn't bash through, it would simply ride up on and break through.[1]

But a politician named George Howlan had the most elegant idea of all. If you couldn't go over the ice, he mused, or through it, why not go under it? Build a subway, he suggested, big enough to run a train through. A true link to the mainland. One you could rely on.

Howlan could back his idea with an impressive list of credentials. In the 1860s, he'd been one of the most powerful members of the House of Assembly. Representing a Prince County district, he was an orator of considerable accomplishment — nicknamed "The Great Wind From the West."[2] He'd also been the acknowledged leader of the Assembly's Roman Catholic faction. From time immemorial — or at least since 1830, when they got the vote — the Island's Roman Catholics had allied themselves with whatever party happened to be for land reform and against the Tories. In 1870, George Howlan turned Island politics on its ear when he led his faction across the floor to join the formerly despised Tories[3].

In 1871, he topped this achievement by spearheading the movement for a Prince Edward Island railway.[4] Eighteen months later, when the railway had the Island teetering on the brink of bankruptcy, he participated in the negotiations to lead the chastened Colony into confederation with Canada. Perhaps unsurprisingly, his electorate rewarded him by rejecting his offer to be their first Member of Parliament in Ottawa. Days after this defeat, his recently-acquired good friend John A. Macdonald appointed him to the Senate.

The Senate was supposed to be the Canadian version of the House of Lords. "A house of sober, second thought." Instead, it was just plain

---

[1] Although some of these ideas were later incorporated into modern icebreakers, shipyards in 1885 didn't have the technology to build a hull strong enough to take that sort of pounding.

[2] Not to be confused with a recently retired member of the House, who was known as "The Great West Wind."

[3] The reasons for this are complex enough to fill another, entire book. Suffice it to say that, after fifteen years of arguing bitterly over whether or not the Island's public school system was or was not Protestant, and whether or not the Colony's Catholics should or should not have their own separate-but-equal schools, the Legislature's Roman Catholic Members realized they hated their own party more than they did their traditional enemies — the Tories.

[4] Convinced that a railroad would be the economic saviour of the Colony, Howlan left no stone unturned and, apparently, few Members unbribed, in his efforts to push the Railway Act through the Legislature.

boring. For a born intriguer like Howlan, it must have been purgatory. The tunnel concept was something he could sink his teeth into. And, perhaps, make a few dollars from. He tackled it with the fervour of a bull terrier.

A railway tunnel was more than a great idea, he argued. It was the Island's right as a member of the federation. "Continuous steam communication" — that's what Ottawa had promised as part of the package that lured Prince Edward Island into Confederation. But the iceboats weren't "steam." And the winter steamship service obviously wasn't "continuous." The tunnel was the only way Ottawa could "maintain, untarnished, that which was of more value than gold, — the honour of the country!"

Not only was a tunnel our right, he continued, it would be our economic salvation. "We would never be imprisoned in the future as we have been in the past," he proclaimed. "Not only will the old industries in this province be stimulated, but quite a large number of new industries will be inaugurated.... For every farmer on the Island there might be three." More linen and wool, he promised. More horses, more cattle, more sheep. Why, Georgetown would surpass Montreal as a port as soon as shippers realized they could bypass the entire treacherous Gulf of St. Lawrence, and transship their goods by train. Through the new Northumberland Strait Subway.

The subway itself was a simple thing. Precast iron and concrete tubes, each one hundred yards long, would be floated out, sunk to the bottom, then bolted together. The great engineer, Sir Douglas Fox, had already built several of the world's longest submarine tunnels, and he was interested in this one. It could be built for between $5 million and $11 million, he estimated, depending on how wide it had to be. This was the most telling argument, tunnel boosters felt. By 1885, with the completion of the Canadian Pacific Railway, the Dominion government had spent over $75 million just to connect a few grumpy British Columbians with the rest of the country. A mere five or ten million, to keep the very cradle of confederation contented, didn't seem like much. It all made so much sense.

There were, however, a few doubters. "A subway!" scoffed a prominent Liberal newspaper. "They cannot get a special train to carry our winter mails, yet we have men simple enough to think they will give us a subway!" And although the electorate agreed that a subway was a grand idea, they made the mistake of returning a full slate of Liberals while the rest of the country elected a Conservative government in 1887. This government looked very seriously at the subway concept, then decided that a new, improved winter steamer would more than complete their constitutional obligations.

Deterred, Howlan and the subway supporters were by no means defeated. In 1891 they returned, with a new improved concept. Technology had progressed, they argued. A subway tunnel, they conceded to their critics, sitting on the floor of the Strait, was in danger of ice damage — especially if the icepan happened to touch bottom in the wrong place. Technology now allowed the construction of a true tunnel — bored *under* the floor of the Strait. Much more sensible. And economical, too. They could prove it. If they were given control of the Prince Edward Island Railroad, part of the annual steamship subsidy, and a complete monopoly, they promised to build the tunnel, operate it, and generate a profit for their shareholders. By 1940, the whole shebang would be paid off.

"We Must Have It!" rang the slogan during the election of 1891. "We Must Have It!" declared the buttons during the election of 1894. "We Must Have It!" moaned discouraged tunnel supporters in 1900. And 1904. And 1908. And 1911.

The tunnel soon slipped into the realm of election lore. Every four years or so, whenever the country went to the polls, the idea of a tunnel to link the Island to the mainland would surface. Every four years or so, candidates would agree that a tunnel sounded like a great idea. Every four years or so, after the election was over, the idea would be shelved — until the next election season. Occasionally, a new, improved steamship would appear in its stead. In 1917, it looked like the idea was dead for good. That's the year the Island finally got the steamship of its dreams — the SS *Prince Edward Island* — our first true icebreaker.

But there are some ideas you can't kill with a stick. The possibility of a tunnel resurfaced in 1941, after the *Charlottetown* sank. In the 1960s, Islanders came *this close* to throwing a causeway across to the mainland. In the 1980s, the idea of a tunnel came back again. It soon metamorphosized into a bridge. Despite great controversy, it's due to open in 1997.

Somewhere, George Howlan is grinning.

Staunch and Strong: SS Prince Edward Island

hough she's little remembered, the *Prince Edward Island* was probably the single most significant boat in Island history. She was certainly the longest-lived. And the hardest-working.

Slab-sided and bluff-bowed, with four ungainly smokestacks sticking out of her upper decks — she was certainly no beauty. But unlike all her predecessors, she had no need to fear the ice. One of the first true ice-breakers in the world, she was designed to smash through, not dance around, the winter ice pack.

Right from the beginning, SS *Prince Edward Island* suffered from a lack of respect. In 1917, when there were delays in her shakedown schedule, grave doubts began to circulate about her reliability. She was shedding rivets by the bucketful every time she even glanced against the ice, one rumour went. Water was pouring into the hull every time she ventured from dock. Why, it was amazing she was even able to make it across the Atlantic, she was so badly put together!

Things got so bad that her master, Captain Murchison, felt he had to make a public defence of his new boat. Murchison was a veteran of the winter steamer service. The old *Earl Grey*, he recalled, had leaked twice as bad — the old *Stanley* was even worse. Why, the *Earl Grey* had once needed ten thousand replacement rivets to get through one winter. One spring back in the 1890s, he'd spent six weeks with a forward hold full of water in the *Stanley*. The *Prince Edward Island* was by far the best boat he'd commanded. "As staunch and strong as the day she came out of the old country," he declared.

She had no need to fear the ice.

There were, however, some minor flaws. Someone in the design office had decided that hot water might be an effective ice-breaking tool. So they ran pipes from the boiler room to the bow to melt the ice with hot water. Fairly useless, Murchison conceded, although handy for washing the snow away. Far better was the forward propeller — excellent for chewing up tough ice pans. The *Prince Edward Island*, he was confident, would be the most reliable boat ever put on the winter run.[1]

Most of the stories in circulation were idle rumour-mongering — a favourite wartime pastime. One complaint, though, suggested there was a fundamental misunderstanding of what sort of boat the *Prince Edward Island* was. Hasn't anyone noticed, asked one puzzled

[1] She was certainly the largest and most powerful. Her engines were rated at over 7,000 horsepower, and she was longer than a football field — a CFL field at that.

Charlottetonian, that the new winter boat didn't really fit the docks at either Charlottetown or Summerside? Government steamers had always shuttled up and down the coastline. What good was a new, improved winter steamer, if it couldn't call at the Island's two major ports?

The *Prince Edward Island* was only going to have two destinations: Cape Tormentine and the brand-new town of Borden.[2] More a part of the railway than the shipping fleet, her main job was to shuttle rail cars across the Northumberland Strait. Few Islanders realized the implications. The *Prince Edward Island* wasn't their new winter steamer. It was their first car ferry. It would revolutionize their transportation system.

The most immediate impact was on the iceboats. Even with the introduction of "winter" steamers in the 1870s, there was still a need for iceboat service. Steamers like the *Earl Grey* and *Stanley* might have been "winterized," but they weren't winterproof. Virtually every season there was a stretch of weather that kept the steamers bottled up in port, and the Island would fall back on the iceboats. The *Prince Edward Island* put them on shore for good.

Second to feel the impact was the railway. By 1917, the Island's rail system was a splendid anachronism. It had been built in 1872 using a light, narrow gauge rail system[3]. Although the rest of the continent had long since switched to the heavier, wider, standard gauge, the Island railway saw no need. Since mainland trains couldn't get onto the Island, why go to the expense of upgrading the rail system to accommodate them? But with the *Prince Edward Island* the pressure was on to standardize the system. Which was done — at great expense — through the 1920s.

A third impact was on the Island's traditional ports. The *Prince Edward Island* allowed the railroad to capture more and more of the province's passenger and freight traffic. Once-bustling waterfronts in Charlottetown, Summerside and Georgetown went into rapid decline. The stevedores' union — once the biggest in the province — faded

---

[2] Since the community's existence sprang out of the ferry terminal, and the ferry terminal was courtesy of Prime Minister Borden, the citizens decided to name the place in his honour.

[3] Rails in a narrow gauge railroad were set 3 feet, 6 inches apart. Standard gauge roads set rails 4 feet, 8 1/2 inches apart. Even when the Prince Edward Island Railway was being built, standard gauge was far more common. But narrow gauge was cheaper, so the Island opted for it. After the system was converted to standard gauge, an Islander was heard to boast: "Our railroad might not be as long as the CPR, but it's just as wide!"

away. But what was probably the major impact was completely unforeseen. The car ferry laid the Island open to the assault of the automobile.

When the *Prince Edward Island* was on the draughting table, most Island roads allowed only limited access to automobiles. Although wartime eased these restrictions considerably, the spring of 1917 still saw long stretches of major highways closed to motorists on certain days. But after the war, all roads were thrown open, and a flood of motorcars began.

This was something the designers of SS *Prince Edward Island* hadn't foreseen. They intended her to be a *rail*car ferry — not a *motor*car ferry. Automobiles could load on her decks, but it was a cumbersome process. If you were a motorist coming to the ferry terminal in, say, 1929, you would first drive onto a flatcar. Your vehicle would be strapped down, and when the flatcar was full a shunting engine would load you on the boat. On the other side, you would wait for the engine to shunt you off, and then carefully drive off the flatcar. Not as clumsy as with some boats, where automobiles had to be hoisted on by a crane, but not very satisfactory.

It was this inability to satisfy the demands of the automobile that drove the *Prince Edward Island* to what was intended to be an early retirement. Plans were on the table for an exciting, new, icebreaking motor and railcar ferry — the *Charlottetown*. When this boat was launched in 1931, the *Prince Edward Island* was relegated to a backup role. Even though she was only fourteen years old, the assumption was that she would soon be in a scrap yard.

The Depression probably saved her. A sister boat to the *Charlottetown* had to wait for better times. Then came the Second World War, with its accompanying material and shipping shortages. Then came her big break. *Charlottetown* sank while en route to a routine refit. Suddenly, the *Prince Edward Island* was back in the spotlight.

Just like her first time around, *Prince Edward Island* got no respect. Frantic business groups and government officials fired appeals to Ottawa to somehow come up with a better boat. The battered hull and faltering engines of the "poor old" *Prince Edward Island* couldn't possibly make it through the winter. The Island was on the verge of being thrown back to the era of the iceboats.

But with a refit that beefed up her engines, and modifications that allowed automobiles to drive straight on, the *Prince Edward Island* was up to the challenge. She served alone, throughout the war and for two years afterwards. In 1947 she was joined on the run by a glamourous new ferry — the *Abegweit*. They let the schools out to celebrate the arrival of the *Abegweit*. The most powerful ice-breaker of her time, beautifully designed and finished, the "*Abby*" quickly won the hearts of every Islander. Once again, the poor old *Prince Edward Island* was pushed into the background.

Twenty years later, in 1967, SS *Prince Edward Island* celebrated her fiftieth birthday — still in service. Given that fifty years of bashing through the pack ice was a lot of strain for any vessel, plans were afoot to replace her. Two years later she made her last trip on the Tormentine-Borden run. It wasn't a retirement, though. Call it a career change.

She was turned into a power hulk. Her deckhouses were cut away — her cabins were ripped out, her engines removed. Huge generators were installed on her car decks, so other boats could moor nearby and plug in. She went to work on the St. Lawrence Seaway. Sort of a giant floating battery. It might not have been pretty, but a job's a job. Some time around — ironically enough — her sixty-fifth birthday, the *Prince Edward Island* was retired for good.

I may well have been the last Islander to ever set foot on SS *Prince Edward Island*. In 1986, while I was going to the University of Toronto, someone told me she was still afloat — well, sort of afloat — at a sort of "old boats' home" in Whitby. I couldn't resist. With instructions from a friend on how to use a GO train, I toddled off to see her.

I found her in a swampy backwater, looming over a bunch of derelict barges and lake boats. She was just a hulk, listing slightly, as much sitting in the mud as floating by the dock. All you could see of her upper works were the cut lines where the torches had swept her clean. The huge generators had been removed from below, so you could see the steel rails imbedded in the deck again. But even though she had more rust than paint left. And even though there was a good dozen feet of water in her hold. And even though she was reduced to little more than the hull that had slid down the slipway back in 1917, she still had an air of dignity about her.

She'd been there a while. It looked like she'd soon be more a part of the lake bank than anything else. So much dirt had accumulated in the companionways that ten-foot alders were growing up her sides.

Fitting, isn't it? What else was there for the hardest-working boat in Island history to do in retirement, than take up gardening?

The Wild Man of Maine

ecember 6, 1913. The hottest ticket of the social season. "Joseph Knowles — The Wild Man of the Maine Woods" was coming live to the People's Theatre. "Clad in the garb of the wild, his stalwart form draped with deer and bear skins, and the bare (get it? — bear/bare?) skin of his tattooed and muscular torso," Knowles the Wild Man would show Charlottetonians how he had triumphed over nature using nothing but his keen wits and lightening quick reflexes. One night only. Adults, 20¢ — children, 15¢. Reserved seats for a quarter.

"A Magnificent Specimen of Manhood," a buck-naked Knowles had entered the Maine woods in August determined to prove that modern man was still fit to survive in a state of nature. He fought his "strenuous battle for existence" armed with nothing but "his bare hands, his knowledge of nature and his remarkable vitality and determination." His tattooed and muscular torso also came in handy.

By all accounts, the magnificent specimen delivered a pretty good show. In his lecture, Knowles described how he built a lean-to, lived on berries and foraged for wild roots and vegetables. After surprising a deer while drinking, he killed it and was naked no more.

Emboldened by his triumph over the deer, he set his sights on bagging a bear. After carefully digging a pit with sharp sticks and stones — which, admittedly, took some considerable time — he hid behind a nearby bush and waited for a bear to fall in. As soon as one obliged, the Wild Man sprang upon it with a hornwood club, tanned its hide and fashioned the very ensemble he was wearing to that night's performance.

As per an agreement with a local Maine paper, Knowles transcribed his thoughts and adventures on birchbark, using bits of charcoal for a pencil. These he left regularly at a pre-arranged tree to be retrieved and transcribed for posterity. After two months of non-stop survival, the Wild Man returned to civilization, an exclusive interview with his sponsoring newspaper, and an international speaking tour.

After the lecture, Knowles showed some slides of the sketches he'd worked up to illustrate some of his adventure's high-points, and topped off the evening by showing some film re-enactments his production company had done. As a finale, he offered to demonstrate his bare-handed, bear-hunting techniques the very next morning — provided anyone in the audience happened to have a spare bear they could lend him.

As it turned out, someone did. Well, sort of. A man named Reg Fraser stood up and allowed that, while he himself was bearless, he did know a fellow up Tignish way who had one. He'd bought it off a trapper in New Brunswick. Like Knowles, this bear was an experienced performer, having appeared recently at the Provincial Exhibition. Would it do?

It would indeed! That night, Knowles worked out the details. He would rise early the next morning, travel to a field north of the City, and dig a pit per his preferred method. When the bear arrived — it was being shipped by overnight express — it would be deposited in the pit. Then, for the safety of the spectators, it would be anchored there with logs and large rocks.

At this point, Knowles would jump in with the bear. He planned to wear clothes this time because: the event was to be filmed, there might be ladies present and it was, after all, the 7th of December. Wielding a club of indeterminate wood species — hornwood being foreign to Prince Edward Island — he would then despatch the bear, proving once again man's inherent superiority over nature. For the safety of the spectators, it was agreed that several sharpshooters would stand by. Mustering the local militia unit was suggested, but declined as being unsporting.

Early the next morning, things began to go awry. Knowles failed to rise early enough to dig his pit with sticks. Besides, on arriving at the field he found the ground was semi-frozen and impervious to all but pick and shovel. A shallow hole was prepared and the logs and large rocks were made ready. The spectators gathered. The camera crew loaded their film. The sharpshooters loaded their weapons.

He offered to demonstrate his bare-handed, bear-hunting techniques.

The bear was late.

The train from Tignish, running on the Prince Edward Island Railway's standard schedule, was behind, as usual. By the time the bear was unloaded and transported to the killing field, it was late in the afternoon. The cameraman declared there was too little light to shoot by. Knowles decided not to waste a good hand-killing if he couldn't get decent footage. Since it was too dark to film on the ground, he suggested letting the bear loose to climb a tree or something, and then film it being shot by the sharpshooters.

At this point common sense intervened. The bystanders pointed out that, once freed, the bear might decide to climb *them*, instead of a tree. They also reminded Knowles that none of the sharpshooters had remembered to bring rifles. They only had shotguns. A shotgun on a bear would have about as much effect as it would on the main hull of a dreadnought. Knowles agreed, and salvaged at least something by agreeing to buy the bear. If he couldn't kill it, he could take it on the rest of his speaking tour.

As if the day hadn't been bad enough, when the Wild Man got back to his hotel he was confronted by a steely-eyed *Patriot* reporter. The *Patriot* heard rumours, spread by a rival paper to Knowles', that the entire affair was a fraud.

The alleged bear-pit was investigated, and judged too shallow to hold a bear, the reporter charged.

It rained. The hole shrank, Knowles replied.

The bear skin robes had bullet holes in them, the reporter accused.

I used a very sharp stick, Knowles replied.

The birchbark notepaper looks to have been cut with a knife, the reporter indicted.

I used a very sharp stone, Knowles replied.

The charcoal letters look to have been traced over with pencil, the reporter inferred.

What utter piffle, Knowles replied.

Your speaking tour is making you $700 to $1000 a week, the reporter fumed.

I work hard for every penny, Knowles stated flatly, ending the interview.

His trying day at an end, the Wild Man of Maine gathered up his gear, and his brand-new bear, and boarded a train for his next speaking engagement.

1918

*In view of the prevalence of influenza in this City,
and in order to prevent its further spread, churches, schools
and theatres will be closed until further notice.*

— Charlottetown Board of Health, October 6, 1918

October 1918 should have been a time of optimism, celebration and relief on Prince Edward Island. After four years of setback and disappointment, the long, bloody war in Europe was approaching conclusion. The armies of darkness and evil[1] were crumbling before the forces of goodness and light.[2] Delighting in reports of frequent and crushing victories in the field, Islanders were savouring the taste of triumph, and musing whether the defeated Kaiser should be hanged, or merely thoroughly humiliated. The bells and proclamations were dusted off in anticipation. A victory celebration of epic proportions was in sight.

Then nature stepped in and spoiled the party.

It's been called the Spanish flu — even though no one has ever been able to explain what was particularly "Spanish" about it. It would start off as an innocent illness. The symptoms were similar to those of a bad cold: headache, coughing, sore throat, runny nose, sneezing, chills, aches and pains, fever and "general physical depression." But it had a nasty habit of turning quickly to pneumonia. In an era before antibiotics, this was a deadly complication.

It had made its debut the previous spring in Central Europe. By summertime it had moved into Western Europe and was filtering across the Atlantic. Because of wartime censorship, it travelled in silence. No nation

---

[1] The German Empire and its allies.
[2] The British Empire and its allies — i.e., us.

wanted to admit how serious individual epidemics had been. By late September the first cases began to appear on Prince Edward Island.

Since "flue" epidemics were nothing new — and because no one had been told what this particular flu was capable of — not much attention was paid to it at first. When it became obvious that it was spreading wider and faster than previous outbreaks, the Charlottetown Board of Health took the precaution of closing churches, schools and theatres. The local press took the precaution of calming the populace.

By 1918, newspapers had given up any pretence to being dispassionate observers of events. They considered themselves an essential part of the war effort — just as vital as a bullet factory. Their job was to keep the citizenry focused on victory. They regarded the spreading epidemic as a minor distraction. Their message? "Don't Panic."

"We understand that there are about 100 cases in the City at present," the *Guardian* noted on October 8. "While there is nothing to be alarmed over, the weather at present is such as to necessitate all possible precautions. With better weather conditions the disease will no doubt disappear as it has done on previous occasions. In the meantime, prudence dictates care, avoidance of unnecessary exposure to cold or wet and a general curbing of imagination which is liable to exaggerate things."

Unfortunately, imagination was hard to curb in the face of this particular flu. Unlike traditional epidemics, which tended to hit the very young and the very old, the Spanish flu selected its victims from the twenty- to forty-year-olds — usually regarded as the hardiest members of society. More alarming was its virulence — its deadliness was matched only by its swiftness.

Frank Cameron, "the well-known and highly efficient teller of the Bank of Commerce," was a typical case. He felt ill on Sunday, but went into work on Monday. There was, after all, a war to be won. By Wednesday he was too sick to continue at work. By Thursday evening he was bad enough to go to the hospital. By Sunday afternoon he was dead. He was twenty-five years old.

As cases like Frank Cameron's began to accumulate, rumours began to run wild. The most common one was that the disease was a secret weapon crafted by German scientists in a desperate attempt to stave off defeat. By October 10, even unaffected communities were deciding — "in order to be on the safe side" — to follow Charlottetown's lead in closing churches and schools. It didn't seem to help, and the epidemic soon spread across the province. As the death toll mounted, daily rou-

The epidemic soon spread across the province.

tines ground to a halt. People were advised to stay indoors. Public health officials were urging that "unnecessary gatherings of people about stores, street corners, etc." also be banned. The flu was slowly shutting down the whole Island.

The patriotic press was enraged. "Here today we have an undue prevalence of bad cold," railed the *Guardian*, "But the name given this bad cold is malignant in itself — Spanish Influenza, and we immediately take fright and refuse to 'carry on'! Remove fear and Spanish Influenza will vanish as quickly as it came." Did the "Boys in Flanders" get a day off from the trenches because of a few sniffles? The same flu had hit England earlier in the summer, for instance, but, "She refused to consider it an infectious disease — She refused to call it 'epidemic' — She refused to interfere with entertainments, meetings, gatherings of business of any kind."[3] That the Island's war effort could be lessened because of a bad cold with a fancy name was almost treasonous!

Perhaps the editors should have read their own obituary pages. A quick glance would have shown them —

Nan Downey — a nurse at the Prince Edward Island Hospital. Dead nine days after falling ill. Age twenty-eight. Before the epidemic had run its course, two doctors and several more nurses would die.

Mrs. Horace Smith — a mother of five young children. Her husband was a soldier recovering from wounds in England.

Mary Margaret Berrigan — "A most estimable young woman who had many friends here." Age twenty-seven.

James Trainor — "skilful and genial barber" left a wife and five children. Age thirty-six.

Walter Leslie left a wife and small child. His brother had died at Vimy Ridge. At Park Corner, George Campbell — "Happy George," as his friends called him — died on a Wednesday. Three days later his youngest son, George Jr., followed him to the grave. Daniel Martell of Georgetown lost his wife and two daughters in the space of a week. Miss Minnie MacLeod of Charlottetown was just eighteen years old. She died on the eve of her wedding day.

The doctors were almost helpless. "Rest, warmth and quiet are the three sovereign remedies of disease," was their best advice. Gargle with diluted quinine — although best known as a cure for malaria, it was the only "miracle drug" around. Take aspirin — as many as you could afford at 25¢ a dozen. Hot poultices might help. So might prayer.

The best remedy was to avoid getting sick at all. The best way to do this was to avoid contact with anyone who might be infected. On

---

[3] She also refused to admit that several hundred thousand of her citizens had died from it.

October 23, as the epidemic peaked in Charlottetown, the Board of Health took the unprecedented step of banning public funerals and ordered that "the bodies of all those dying of influenza and pneumonia must be buried within 24 hours." In a community that had traditionally taken great comfort in the rituals of the public wake, this was a desperate measure indeed.

Even though cases continued throughout the winter, by mid-November the epidemic had run its course. But Island families still weren't immune. As the epidemic worked its way across the continent, telegrams began to arrive advising that a son had died in Toronto, a daughter in Calgary. By the time it was done, Spanish influenza killed over four hundred Islanders.

Smallpox, cholera, typhoid, diphtheria — Prince Edward Island was visited at one time or another by all of the classic killers. None had a fraction of the power of the 1918 epidemic. Brute numbers tell the tale. Four hundred Islanders died in the epidemic — the same number killed by the war. Nation-wide, the flu claimed 55,000, compared to 60,000 war dead. World-wide, it took the ingenuity and accumulated treasure of five empires four years of warfare to kill 10 million people. The flu killed 25 million in a mere eight months.

If it had struck at any other time in history, the Spanish Influenza would be remembered in all its searing intensity. But since it occurred at the climax of the bloodiest war in history, it was forgotten even as it was happening. Perhaps its stunning swiftness helped to blunt the senses. Or perhaps no one wanted to dwell on the notion that a mere "bug" could wield such power — even over the most "advanced" of societies.

Scares the willies out of me.

The Wreck of The Charlottetown

he was the pride of the Island. Built in 1931, she was the most powerful ice breaker of her era. Over 300 long, displacing 5,900 tons, she was our first custom-built car-ferry. Her skipper was one of the finest mariners in the province — Captain John Read of Summerside. She wasn't exactly a *pretty* boat, but she was widely beloved. Because, from the day of her launch, the *Charlottetown* was our main link with the mainland.

On June 18, 1941, the *Charlottetown* was somewhere between Halifax and Liverpool, Nova Scotia. She had been removed from her routine run for a refit in Saint John. It was very foggy. The lookout was inexperienced and the waters were unfamiliar. Captain Read, though, was steaming as close to shore and making as much speed as he could. On the face of it, this must have seemed foolhardy. But it was wartime and the Nova Scotia coast was part of a battleground. Although the papers whispered not a word, mariners knew that German U-boats were ranging up to the mouth of Halifax harbour and that these were not secure waters. Captain Read was trusting luck and his lookout to get the *Charlottetown* safely through.

Suddenly, pelting along at a full twelve knots, the boat hit something — no one knew what. Chief Engineer Dalziel heard a sound: "like the ripping of canvas, only a hundred times louder." Someone yelled: "My God! That's rock!" as the deck crew tore below to see what happened. They found water pouring into the hull, but couldn't find the hole. The first wave doused the boilers, and the wounded ferry drifted to a stop.

Captain Read didn't seem that worried, at first. He told one of his Mates to take a boat ashore and telephone Halifax to ask for a tug. Read could have radioed ashore, but with the *Charlottetown* dead in the water, he wasn't willing to take the chance a German submarine might be listening.

The Company's office in Halifax wasn't as reluctant to break radio silence. As soon as the Mate got through, they radioed back with bad news. The closest tugboat was two days away. They suggested Read try and round up another tow.

The closest motorboats belonged to fishermen in a nearby port. After negotiation, eight agreed to come out and put a line aboard the stricken ferry. What a sight that must have been. The *Charlottetown* — 5,900 tons of great, lumbering car ferry, and its team of eight tiny lobster boats. However it looked, it worked. *Charlottetown* was soon underway again.

At this point the Captain and the Chief Engineer began to argue over strategy. Chief Dalziel was convinced the ship was mortally wounded, and urged the Captain to beach her. If the boat was going to sink, he reasoned, make sure it was in shallow water so salvage would be easier. Captain Read was having none of that. He was sure the *Charlottetown* could make it to a drydock, and asked the fishermen to set course for Halifax. Perhaps he was confident, or perhaps he was merely damned if he was going to crown a fine career at sea by running his command onto a sandbar.

Read should have listened to Dalziel. After a few hours, the fishermen began to notice the angle on the tow lines getting lower. The *Charlottetown* was getting heavier, and the ship was beginning to settle. The fishermen had a hurried conference with the Captain. The boat was going down, they said, and if they didn't cut the tow, they were going with her. Read had to agree, and ordered the crew into their own lifeboats. Thirty-six hours after hitting whatever she hit, the *Charlottetown* sank. As it was reckoned she went down a hundred fathoms, there was no hope of refloating her.

Back in her namesake city, all hell broke loose when word of the sinking came out. June 1941 wasn't exactly brimming with good news to make up for it. The war was going terribly. The German Army was pounding the bejesus out of Russia. And though there was no official acknowledgement of the fact, many suspected how the German Navy was pounding the bejesus out Britain shipping. Now the *Charlottetown* — our only reliable link to the mainland — was gone forever. Rumours began to fly. Captain and crew were roaring drunk and couldn't see where they were going, ran one story. No, went another, she was torpedoed. Or chased onto the shoal by a U-boat. Whatever the reason, the loss of the *Charlottetown* was considered a disaster, and someone would have to answer for it.

Eight agreed to come out and put a line aboard the stricken ferry.

Captain Read was the natural choice, and it was soon obvious that his career had gone down with his boat. He got to celebrate New Year's, 1942, by attending the opening of the inquiry into the sinking. He told the Court he was sure the *Charlottetown* ran into a submerged wreck, since his charts showed no shoals or sandbars along the course he had been sailing. The Court countered that the charts were out of date. It further charged that he had been sailing too fast, that he should have radioed immediately for help, and that he'd been "negligent and overconfident" in handling the ship. Read's only possible defence to the latter — that he'd been taking routine precautions against U-boat attack — was never raised. His ticket was suspended for six months. He never sailed again.

The Little Airline
That Could

n the spring of 1940, the Mayor of Summerside got a rather unpleasant letter. It was from the Chief Pilot of Canadian Airways Limited.[1] The tone was cold. The airline intended to put a nifty new aeroplane on the Charlottetown-Summerside-Moncton route. Existing airfield facilities on the Island — especially in Summerside — were barely fit for the present service. They were not at all suitable for the new aircraft. If the community didn't immediately redevelop its airport, the airline was going to drop it from the route.

The letter was probably calculated to insult. Canadian Airways was the largest private airline in the country, and it had decided that its Prince Edward Island connection wasn't generating enough profit. It wanted out. But since CAL was obligated to the Dominion Government to deliver airmail to the Island, it couldn't simply shut down the route. It needed a pretext. The shoddy Summerside airfield was a perfect excuse. The government in Ottawa reluctantly agreed, and CAL flew away for good.[2]

Ottawa now needed someone to provide at least a basic air link to Prince Edward Island. It pressured Trans Canada Airlines[3] to take over the route — which it did

---

[1] CAL was a quiet subsidiary of the Canadian Pacific Railroad. The CPR had a controlling interest in the airline, but preferred not to advertise the fact.

[2] A corporate descendant of CAL — Air Atlantic — returned to the Island in the 1980s.

[3] Trans Canada was the direct ancestor to modern-day Air Canada. TCA was the "government" airline, formed in the early 1930s by — irony of ironies — a Conservative administration. The advantage was that it had first pick of the best routes. The drawback was it could be forced to operate marginal or unprofitable routes when politics dictated.

with extreme reluctance. But there were soon suspicions that TCA had quietly instructed its pilots to look for every possible procedural or mechanical excuse to stay regretfully on the ground in Moncton until nightfall — at which time they would have to cancel the flight. It was obvious that TCA would also soon be looking for a pretext to drop the route. Enter Carl Burke.

Born in Charlottetown in 1913, Burke had caught the bug for flying — bad. In the spring of 1936 he dedicated his $12-a-week salary as a hardware store clerk to paying for an extremely used, $600 aeroplane he'd bought with the help of a friend. And to financing flying lessons. By the fall of the year he had his licence and a small charter business.

He stayed on at the hardware store, but spent most of his lunch hours in the air. Miss the train for Summerside? Have to get to Amherst really fast? Just want to go for a ride? Captain Burke would oblige. He'd fly anywhere, on any errand, just to build up his flight time. In 1939 it paid off, and he landed a pilot's position with CAL.

He was assigned the Moncton-Summerside-Charlottetown run. Though most flights were routine, some were not. One woman remembered having to get to Summerside for her mother's funeral. It was wintertime, and the airfield had too much snow cover to make a safe landing. Burke advised the woman she'd have to land in Charlottetown and take the train. This meant missing the funeral. She pleaded. He improvised.

"He asked would I be willing to jump ten or twelve feet," she recalled, four decades later. "He didn't dare let the pontoons touch as he might not be able to get in the air again. I said I'd try, so they threw my suitcase out and he said: 'Now jump, and good luck.' I prayed to the Lord and made a safe landing. The snow was soft."

Burke was with the airline for little over a year when CAL got permission to drop his route. It offered a job on one of its western routes. He declined. He had a better idea. He wanted to found his own airline. Just a small one to start, based on the Moncton-Summerside-Charlottetown route. He'd call it "Maritime Central Airways" — or MCA. He knew he could make it work.

A friend at Canadian Airways had slipped him a copy of the balance sheet for the route — it had always broken even, and sometimes generated a small profit. Connections within the government in Ottawa advised him that since TCA didn't want the route, he would be guaranteed the airmail contract. Connections within the government in Charlottetown told him that the Premier was not at all happy with the service being provided by TCA, and would be delighted to see an Islander take it over. All he needed was $100,000, more or less, to get off the ground.

Burke himself had about $5,000 in savings. Raising the balance

He asked would I be willing to jump ten or twelve feet.

might have seemed a daunting task. But remember — Carl Burke had once persuaded a passenger to jump out of a moving aeroplane. Drumming up a few tens of thousands of dollars wouldn't be a problem. His pitch was simple. "I would point out that this is the only airline in Canada that is not now in control of a large corporation. All other territory is now licensed and controlled by TCA, CAL, etc." MCA might seem like small potatoes, but it was the only way a small investor could hope to get into the airline business.

By the summer of 1941 he had the money in place. The Department of Transport had issued him a radio frequency. The Post Office had his airmail contract all ready to sign. Pilots from all over the country were writing to see if he might have a job for them. Burke even had a logo ready to go. All he needed was an aeroplane.

The war had made passenger planes — new, used or otherwise — a very precious commodity. After a summer of scouring every corner of the country, Burke finally persuaded the RCAF to sell him a used ten-seater called a Barclay Grow.[4] The Barclay Grow was an ugly aeroplane with a less-than-shining reputation. The Air Force had entirely lost faith in the Grow's ability to aid the war effort, so had no qualms in selling it to MCA. With this and a Boeing 247 as a back-up, Maritime Central Airways was in business. It was December 7, 1941.

Despite the bad omen of starting up the same day as the bombing of Pearl Harbour, MCA performed as Burke had predicted. Small but steady profits began to accumulate. More stops were added to the run — Grindstone, Blissville, Greenwood, Yarmouth, New Glasgow, Halifax, Fredericton and Saint John joined the basic Moncton-Summerside-Charlottetown route. Ironically, success meant less time in the cockpit for Burke himself. When MCA began, he was one of two pilots, flying five times a week in addition to managing the airline. Within a few years he was flying only enough to keep his commercial licence active.[5]

---

[4] Burke actually had an earlier deal to buy a similar aeroplane from a company in Ontario, but this fell through at the last minute. There were dark suspicions that CAL had secretly sabotaged the deal.

[5] By 1950, he had let his commercial licence lapse. In his time, though, he was known as an extremely gifted pilot. In 1941 he served with ATFERO — later known as Ferry Command. ATFERO flew heavy bombers that had been built in North America to their operational bases in Great Britain. This may sound routine today, but in 1941 transatlantic flight was still in its infancy. The flights were gruelling — ten to sixteen hours long — and not every aeroplane made it intact.
He also flew a spectacular rescue mission in 1943. On January 28, an RAF

In 1952 Maritime Central got a tremendous boost, courtesy of the Cold War. The Canadian and American Departments of Defence decided to build a string of early warning radar stations as a caution against possible Soviet air attack. Dubbing it the "Pine Tree Line," they selected MCA as the main air carrier for the eastern portion. Two years later, the airline was able to boast it had lifted 10,000 tons, flown 6 million miles and transported 100,000 people. Not only did the Pine Tree project pay very well, it provided Burke and his airline with priceless experience in airlifting heavy equipment. In 1955, when the Canadian and American governments decided to build the much larger Distant Early Warning Line, MCA was their first choice for civilian air contractor.

The DEW Line was a huge undertaking. A string of fifty radar sites were to be built between Alaska and Baffin Island. Because the sites had to be built quickly, and because many were too far north to be easily accessible, close to half of the material and equipment required had to come in by air. Working conditions were daunting. Ground crew worked in -60° temperatures, out in the open, in unrelenting winds. Aircrew rarely knew if they were landing on land or sea — more than one aircraft sank through what was thought to be a solid runway. MCA would log 28,000 flights in twenty-nine months. Fly close to 5 million miles. Lift 35,000 tons. Only the United States Air Force moved more. In scale, scope and duration, it was one of the biggest airlifts ever undertaken in peacetime. Much larger than the famous Berlin airlift. When it was completed, those who paid the bills sent Burke a note of congratulations: "We do believe that the task you have successfully completed is the toughest assignment ever undertaken by a Canadian commercial carrier."

It was also one of the most lucrative. Of the $350 million budgeted for the project, $45 million was dedicated to the airlift. Twenty-five million went into MCA's bank account. Five million got to stay there. Burke bought a Quebec-based airline, Nordair, with part of the proceeds. This gave him the possibility of extending routes into central Canada. By 1957, Maritime Central Airways was ranked as the country's third-biggest airline — and its single biggest freight carrier.

The Pine Tree and DEW line projects had been challenging, patriotic and profitable. They'd also allowed Burke and MCA to escape

---

training flight crashed on the Gulf of St. Lawrence. The crew of four survived, but were stranded on an ice floe. Burke flew out in a two-seater ski plane and took them off, one by one. Then he went back for the radio. He won an Order of the British Empire for that one.

from the reality of the airline business as it developed in the 1950s. Operating costs were growing. Profit margins were shrinking. Competition was getting downright cutthroat. There was less and less room for small, regional carriers like MCA. The DEW line money was quickly swallowed up. Two years after recording its biggest ever profit, the MCA wrote its biggest loss ever into the books.

Burke had seen these developments, and tried to counter. MCA developed an overseas charter service. "Anything, Anywhere," was its motto. But when the bigger airlines increased their scheduled transatlantic service, the charter market evaporated.[6] MCA opened new routes in the Maritimes. They barely broke even. Nordair opened a "Seaway" route connecting Montreal and Toronto. This lost so much money it closed within a year. A hoped-for expansion into Newfoundland and Labrador was dashed when a competitor — Eastern Provincial Airlines — was awarded the route instead. An innovative "Air Van" programme for moving American servicemen, their families and furniture was a success. As was a contract to clean, refuel and restock international flights when they landed at the Moncton airport. But this was pretty basic work — almost demeaning — for an airline that had just helped save the Free World.

By 1963, Carl Burke decided MCA had run out of room to manoeuvre. An off-hand comment at a business dinner that the airline might be for sale led to serious negotiations. Eastern Provincial — MCA's main competitor — ponied up over $22 million to buy the company's shares. Carl Burke was a pilot. And any pilot knows that when the weather forecast is bad, and the aeroplane's almost out of fuel, only a lunatic would insist on flying on.

---

[6] Burke was also very shaken when an MCA charter crashed near Issodun, Quebec, killing everyone on board. With a death toll of seventy-four, it was the country's worst air disaster to that date. Although the subsequent inquiry found nothing wrong with either the aeroplane or how it was operated, the crash cast a considerable pall over the airline.

Boyde Beck was born in Montague, Prince Edward Island. After deciding that the 1980s were a good time to stay in school, he eventually completed Grade XX at the University of Prince Edward Island, Queens and the University of Toronto. He now works as a Curator at the PEI Museum and Heritage Foundation, and lives in Mount Stewart with his wife, Anna, and their two cats.

P. John Burden's illustrations can be found in many books for both children and grown-ups. Long ago he trained as a line engraver and was irrevocably influenced by his master, Henry Wilkinson. John is also an artist in other media, including traditional stained glass. He and his partner, Robin Bakker, and their daughter Jessie muddle along with various cats, dogs, spiders and rabbit ghosts in and about their home on the banks of the Wheatley River in Prince Edward Island.